Legislative Drafting

Edited by
Aldo Zammit Borda

Routledge
Taylor & Francis Group
LONDON AND NEW YORK

First published 2011
by Routledge
2 Park Square, Milton Park, Abingdon, Oxon, OX14 4RN

Simultaneously published in the USA and Canada
by Routledge
52 Vanderbilt Avenue, New York, NY 10017

Routledge is an imprint of the Taylor & Francis Group, an informa business

This book is a reproduction of *Commonwealth Law Bulletin*, vol. 36, issue 1. The Publisher requests to those authors who may be citing this book to state, also, the bibliographical details of the special issue on which the book was based.

Typeset in Times by Taylor & Francis Books

British Library Cataloguing in Publication Data
A catalogue record for this book is available from the British Library

ISBN13: 978-0-415-59781-4 (hbk)

Disclaimer
The publisher would like to make readers aware that the chapters in this book are referred to as articles as they had been in the special issue. The publisher accepts responsibility for any inconsistencies that may have arisen in the course of preparing this volume for print.

Contents

Articles

Notes on Contributors

St John Bates is the Director of the St John Bates Consultancy (a subsidiary of Bates Enterprises Ltd) which offers legislative drafting services internationally (www.stjohnbatesconsultancy.com), a Visiting Professor at the University of Strathclyde Law School in Scotland and an Associate Senior Research Fellow, Institute of Advanced Legal Studies, University of London.

Duncan Berry is a consultant Parliamentary Counsel at the Irish Office of the Parliamentary Counsel to the Government. He holds an LLM, MPP, GDSM, and SJD. He is also the Secretary of the Commonwealth Association of Legislative Counsel and the editor of the Association's Journal 'TheLoophole'.

VCRAC Crabbe is an expert in the field of legislative drafting and has held a number of high-profile positions, including: Commissioner (Statute Law Revision of Ghana); Professor of Legislative Drafting (University of the West Indies, Cave Hill Campus, Barbados); Director, Commonwealth Secretariat Scheme for Legislative Draftsmen (for the West Africa, East Africa, Southern and Central Africa Regions and the Caribbean Region); First Parliamentary Counsel and Constitutional Adviser (to the Ugandan Government); Chairman (Constituent Assembly for the drafting of the 1979 Constitution for Ghana); Judge (Supreme Court of Ghana) and Senior Instructor (International Law Development Centre, Rome, Italy).

Graham Greenleaf is Professor of Law at the University of New South Wales (UNSW); Andrew Mowbray is Professor of Law at the University of Technology, Sydney (UTS); and Philip Chung is Executive Director of AustLII and Lecturer in Law at the University of Technology, Sydney.

Ranjit Hewagama CBE is a legislative drafting consultant and a consultant with Omar Associates Attorneys-at-Law, Colombo, Sri Lanka. He holds an LLB from the University of Ceylon and has extensive experience in the area of legislative drafting having, amongst others, held the following positions: Assistant Legal Draftsman, Sri Lanka, 1972–1975; Assistant

Parliamentary Counsel, Jamaica, 1975–1978; Parliamentary Counsel, Jamaica, 1978–1985; Legal Draftsman, the Solomon Islands, 1985–2007 (1998–2001 Legal Draftsman/Solicitor General); Chairman, Law Revision Commission, the Solomon Islands; and Member of the Judicial and Legal Services Commission, the Solomon Islands.

Sandra C. Markman is consultant legislative drafter and trainer. For the past year, she has been in Dublin, Ireland, where she is a Consultant Parliamentary Counsel in the Attorney General's Office, drafting legislative instruments as well as developing and delivering training to drafters. A native of Montreal, Ms Markman was called to the Bar there in 1980 and then entered private practice. In 1984, she moved to Ottawa to obtain a Diploma of Legislative Drafting from the University of Ottawa. After her graduation in 1985, she joined the Department of Justice Canada, where she spent 22 years as a legislative drafter and manager. Since 2007, Ms Markman has worked as a consultant in the Caribbean and Europe. For some years, Ms Markman served as an adjunct (part-time) professor in the Faculty of Common Law at the University of Ottawa, teaching legislative drafting and related subjects to undergraduate and graduate law students. In the 1999–2000 academic year she taught full-time as part of an exchange between the University and the Department of Justice. In 2008, she was an Instructor in the course for Parliamentary Counsel offered by the Commonwealth Secretariat in Georgetown, Guyana for Parliamentary Counsel from the Caribbean region. Ms Markman has made presentations on drafting and legislative process issues to officials from Sweden, South Africa, Vietnam, Pakistan, Bangladesh and China. She has also served as an expert for the ILO in Geneva on the preparation of its drafting manual for international instruments.

N.K. Nampoothiry is Joint Secretary and Legislative Counsel at the Ministry of Law and Justice, Government of India, New Delhi and formerly Legal Expert and Advanced Legislative draftsperson, Attorney General's Chambers, Ministry of Legal Affairs, Government of the Co-operative Republic of Guyana, Georgetown.

Richard C. Nzerem is the Hon. Director of the Sir William Dale Centre for Legislative Studies, Institute of Advanced Legal Studies of the University of London. He is also a legal consultant and former Director of the Legal and Constitutional Affairs Division, Commonwealth Secretariat. He holds an LLM (Lond).

Justice Robin Webster MBE has been drafting legislation since the late 1970s, when he joined the Office of the Solicitor to the Secretary of State for Scotland in Edinburgh. Secondments then followed as the Legal Draftsman to the Seychelles Government; Assistant Parliamentary Draftsman in the Lord Advocate's Department in London; Senior Parliamentary Counsel to the Kenya Government; and Attorney-General of the tiny Pacific island state of Tuvalu. He became a Judge of the Supreme Court of Tonga in 1988, being awarded the MBE for services to the judiciary in Tonga. In 1991 he returned home to Scotland and was an Employment Tribunal Chairman for several years. In 2004 he was asked to return to Tonga as Chief Justice, a post he held until 2006. Since then he has been Course Director of the Commonwealth Secretariat Caribbean Short Course in Legislative Drafting in 2007 and 2008.

Foreword

I am delighted that the focus of this special issue of the *Commonwealth Law Bulletin* is on legislative drafting. This area of legal work generally does not get the attention it deserves having regard to the increasingly important role played by statutes in our legal systems.

The Hon Justice Michael Kirby AC CMG (as he then was) in an article published in the Statute Law Review in 2003 wrote:

> The world of common law principle is in retreat. It now circles in the orbit of statute. Where statute speaks – and particularly a curious statute like a Constitution or a Human Rights Act – there is no escaping the duty to give meaning to its words. That is what I, and every other judge in the countries of the world that observe the rule of law, spend most of our time doing.[1]

My own journey along the path of a career in statute law writing began in September 1974 when I joined the Office of the Legislative Draftsmen in Northern Ireland. While at university the previous year I had written a paper that required me to carry out some research into the background of a particular legislative item. Somehow, and I cannot now recall precisely how, I got the opportunity to discuss the matter with Mr William Leitch, a legendary Northern Irish draftsman. From that encounter there must have developed deep within my consciousness the idea that legislative drafting might provide an interesting career choice. By the time an advertisement was published the following year for a junior drafting position in the Belfast office I didn't hesitate to apply and was delighted to be offered the post. I have never regretted the choice I made.

Over the course of my career so much has changed. At its beginning, a draft was prepared in longhand and then typed up by a secretary using a manual typewriter. Changes had to be made either by typing up new slips and pasting them onto the page or by whitening out some text and typing new material in its place. When finalised, drafts were sent to the government printing office which, using hot metal typesetting, produced a printed version. That version, of course, had to be manually proofread against the typed copy. There were no electronic databases of legislation so appropriate precedents, and places where consequential amendments were needed, had to be found by manual searching or recalled from one's own memory bank. Very low down in the scale of things in the mind of the typical drafter, at least in mine, was any conscious advertence to the need for simplicity in writing style. The task was to produce a workable law within the given timeframe using the available resources.

---

[1] 'Towards a Grand Theory of Interpretation: The Case of Statutes and Contracts' (2003) 24(2) Statute Law Review, at 95, 97.

The working world today for the vast majority of legislative drafters is so different. All available relevant technologies are used in the production of texts. Individualised templates maintain consistency in layout. Macros ensure consistency with in-house rules. Computerised search facilities help ensure consistency in word usage. Most jurisdictions have up-to-date electronic versions of their written laws available to their drafters and indeed to everyone through the World Wide Web. Precedents from all over the world can be found in an instant. Revised drafts can be quickly produced and disseminated to clients. For many jurisdictions the final printing process does not involve any proofreading as the same set of data is used throughout. And, when introduced to the legislature, a Bill can be made available to the whole community instantly by uploading it to the internet. It is a very different working environment from that of 1974.

Apart from all the technological changes, legislative drafters have been impacted by changes in the approach to interpreting statutes and, of course, by the plain language movement.

In the course of my career the pendulum has very much swung from a literal to a purposive approach to statutory interpretation. In some jurisdictions this changed approach has been mandated by statute while in others it has been arrived at through judicial development. It has resulted in the situation that courts are prepared to do some work on the text (either by reading words in, omitting words or straining the meaning of words) to ensure that it delivers the meaning that it was apparently intended to bear having regard to the overall context. Way back in 1969 the Law Commissions in Great Britain had recommended a purposive approach[2] and had recognised that the 'intelligibility of statutes from the point of view of ordinary citizens or their advisers cannot in fact be dissociated from the rules of interpretation followed by the courts, for the ability to understand a statute depends in the ultimate analysis on intelligent anticipation of the way in which it would be interpreted by the courts'.[3] This changed approach has made drafters realise the importance of making the purpose underlying the text as clear as possible assisted by the knowledge, in some jurisdictions, that recourse might be had to extrinsic materials to help in that search. However, given the importance of the legislative text as the source of law, it remains the prime responsibility of the legislative drafter to make the purpose underlying it clear. To this end many drafters now make use of purpose clauses, explanatory notes, examples, overviews and other aids to assist the reader in understanding the context and aim of the legislation.

At the same time as this changed approach to interpretation was happening, the spotlight was shining very brightly on the issue of the intelligibility of legislation. A major event was the publication in 1975 in the United Kingdom of the Renton Committee report.[4] While noting that they had discovered that even judges, never mind ordinary citizens, find it difficult to understand legislation,[5] they highlighted some of the difficulties facing legislative drafters:

---

[2]The Interpretation of Statutes (Law Com No 21) (Scot Law Com No 11).
[3]At para 4.
[4]The Preparation of Legislation, May 1975.
[5]At para 7.6.

- the sheer mass of statute law enacted each year dealing with an ever-expanding range of complex situations;
- the impossibility of dealing in simple non-technical terms with technical and complex subjects while at the same time pursuing certainty of legal effect as a primary objective;
- the format of Bills being dictated by political or legislative process considerations;
- the shortage of time available for preparing Bills;
- the under-resourcing of drafting offices accentuated by the difficulties in attracting suitable people as legislative drafters.[6]

The solution that the Renton Committee opted for was to adopt, whenever feasible, a 'general principle' approach to drafting, that is, using statements of principle or broad general rules accompanied, if necessary, by detailed provisions.[7] Lord Denning was an early supporter of this approach. He stated:

> It comes to this, that language ought to be simple and clear. There ought to be not long but short sentences. There should be a few commas and semi-colons in sentences. There should be simple words. There should not be too much detail. One of the troubles is that with the best motives the draftsmen try to think of every contingency … It is impossible to think of everything that will happen in the future. All this ought to be in simple language expressing principles. There is no need to go into all this detail. The courts should then be allowed to deal with it, as I am sure they have in the past.[8]

While a 'general principle' approach to drafting never really took off in common law jurisdictions because of concerns that it failed to deliver the desired degree of certainty and shifted too much responsibility to the courts to determine how legislation applied in particular circumstances, the emphasis on the need for simple language very much remained. In Australia it was given much impetus by the work of the Law Reform Commission of Victoria from 1985 to 1992.[9]

In an article published in 2001 in the *Statute Law Review*,[10] Professor Ruth Sullivan emphasised that plain language drafting goes beyond issues relating to vocabulary and syntax to encompass internal organisation, document design and the use of appropriate reader aids. She observed that plain language drafters 'pay as much attention to fonts and white space as they do to choice of words'.[11]

As a result of all these developments, the scope of a legislative drafter's task has considerably broadened. Yet the difficulties facing legislative drafters highlighted by the Renton Committee still remain. Indeed they have been added to.

---

[6]See Chapters VII and VIII.
[7]At para 10.13.
[8]United Kingdom, *Parliamentary Debates*, House of Lords, 15 December 1982, col 617.
[9]See its reports *Plain English and the Law* published in June 1987 and *Access to the Law: The Structure and Format of Legislation* published in 1990.
[10]'Some Implications of Plain Language Drafting (2001) 22(3), 175.
[11]At 175.

Considerations related to human rights and the rule of law have emphasised the need for law to be 'accessible'. Thus in *Sunday Times v United Kingdom*[12] the European Court of Human Rights referred to the requirements that flowed from the expression 'prescribed by law' in Article 10 of the European Convention on Human Rights. It stated:

> Firstly, the law must be adequately accessible: the citizen must be able to have an indication that is adequate in the circumstances of the legal rules applicable to a given case. Secondly, a norm cannot be regarded as a 'law' unless it is formulated with sufficient precision to enable the citizen to regulate his conduct: he must be able – if need be with appropriate advice – to foresee, to a degree that is reasonable in the circumstances, the consequences which a given action may entail.

Such considerations make the role played by the legislative drafter all the more critical. A failure to produce a readily comprehensible law may in particular circumstances lead to invalidity and not just uncertainty.

Clearly the job of a legislative drafter is an important one. What qualities do you need to be able to perform it competently? Apart from the obvious requirement of a good solid legal education I would suggest that you require a love of language, the capacity for clear thought, high-level problem-solving skills, the ability to see the big picture as well as to hone in on the finest detail and the possession of a thick skin. You will need the latter to be able to deal with all the criticism liable to be heaped on your work by judges, politicians, academics, other lawyers and indeed just about everyone else. An interest in politics (short of partisanship) and current affairs generally can also prove useful.

On commencing a career in legislative drafting you have a lot of new things to learn. You need to develop a deep familiarity with the terms of the local Interpretation legislation. This is a statute that you may never have heard of as you moved through law school. Yet legislative drafters assume knowledge of it in their readers. Thus a term that is defined there (for example, document) will not be defined in any other legislation that uses the term. Readers are expected to be aware of the definition. There are also interesting rules to be found in Interpretation legislation about the exercise of powers, the calculation of time, the effect of repeals and a raft of other matters.

You need to become familiar with the rules of parliamentary procedure and how they impact on the presentation of Bills and their capacity to be amended. You need to develop an overall good knowledge of the local statute-book as any new law must be woven within it as seamlessly as possible. To write criminal laws you need to be familiar with criminal procedure and with the sentencing structure of courts. There are other areas, for example, general government financial legislation, of which you need to develop some knowledge. Through gaining this specialised knowledge you become an expert in the development of legislative schemes and can counsel and advise the proponents of new schemes. A fully-fledged legislative drafter is not merely someone who puts words on a page but a person capable of performing an important advisory role. Not infrequently, for the policy colleagues on a drafting project it is their first legislative experience, and

---

[12] (1979–80) 2 EHRR 245.

they are very much in need of guidance and assistance from an experienced hand at such projects.

Clearly there is a real need for those setting out on a drafting career to be adequately trained. Traditionally the emphasis has been on in-house, on-the-job training. While some external courses are available,[13] a lack of resources can prevent them being accessible to drafters in under-resourced jurisdictions. Unfortunately there tends to be a great disparity in the resources available to legislative drafters across jurisdictions and yet the essential task to be performed remains the same.

Attendance at international drafting conferences is a valuable source of learning about particular aspects of legislative drafting. Such conferences are organised by the Commonwealth Association of Legislative Counsel (CALC) in conjunction with each Commonwealth Law Conference. The most recent one was held in Hong Kong, China in April 2009. The formal conference programme usually extends over $2^1/_2$ days and allows detailed discussion on a range of drafting-related topics. The next CALC conference will be held in India, in 2011. Regional drafting conferences are also regularly organised by the Canadian Institute for the Administration of Justice (CIAJ) and by the Australasian Parliamentary Counsel's Committee. In April 2010, CALC is holding an Africa Region Conference in Abuja, Nigeria.

The objects of CALC include the promotion of co-operation on matters of common interest among Commonwealth drafters and the dissemination of information about legislative drafting, and the role of those who engage in it. CALC provides a valuable networking forum for legislative drafters. From its formation in 1983, CALC has grown to an organisation with around 1000 members drawn from some 100 jurisdictions. It publishes a flagship journal, *The Loophole*, as well as regular Newsletters. Its website at http://www.opc.gov.au/calc/index.htm is an excellent resource for information about, and articles related to, legislative drafting. CALC has recently joined forces with CIAJ to provide an online forum facility for CALC members to discuss matters of mutual interest.

As highlighted in this Foreword, the changes over the course of my 35 year drafting career have been immense. They have involved not only changes to the tools available to do the work, but also changes in the techniques used in doing it. What changes lie ahead in the course of the next 35 years? It really is impossible to predict this with any real hope of accuracy. The move from seeing legislation as a paper product to seeing it as an on-line product is likely to continue and gain pace. This may well impact on the writing and presentation style used. The on-line product also opens up opportunities for hypertext links to cross-referenced texts enabling the presentation of a more comprehensive package. Some governments may also seek community involvement in drafting projects through the use of a wiki. This has been trialled in New Zealand on police legislation and the Australian Government in 2009 expressed some interest in it. While such exercises do generate community involvement in what should be covered by legislation, they fail (at least superficially) to recognise that legislative drafting is a skilled art and that not every member of the community can practise it.

---

[13]Details about available courses can be found on the website of the Commonwealth Association of Legislative Counsel at http://www.opc.gov.au/calc/training.htm.

However in my view, despite the heavy demands placed on legislative drafters, the intrinsic difficulty of their task, the all-too-frequent criticism directed at their product and the limited resources with which many have to carry out their work, legislative drafting is still the best legal job going. I hope that, after having read the articles contained in this Special Issue, you will gain some insight into the world of the legislative drafter and what makes drafting such an attractive career choice.

Eamonn Moran, PSM QC JP
President, Commonwealth Association of Legislative Counsel
Law Draftsman, Hong Kong Special Administrative Region, China
Hong Kong, 1 November 2009

Preface

I am deeply honoured to have been asked by the Editor, Dr Aldo-Zammit Borda to write the preface to this Special issue of the *Commonwealth Bulletin* which on this occasion exclusively features legislative drafting as its theme. As the new Director of the Legal and Constitutional Affairs Division (LCAD), I recognise the privilege and responsibility that follows from having accepted the invitation and have therefore decided to use this opportunity wisely to showcase the remarkable institutional and capacity building work done since 1974 by the Commonwealth Secretariat in support of legislative drafting in general and legislative draftspersons in particular.

The long tradition of Secretariat engagement in this important area of work can be traced back to the first Secretary-General of the Commonwealth, Arnold Smith, who noted in his book *Stitches in Time* that the Secretariat's 'primary function was to provide information about legislation in Commonwealth countries … [including through] the launching of an ambitious publication, the Commonwealth Law Bulletin'. Smith went on to note that 'another logical advance was to inaugurate a series of training courses for parliamentary draftsmen'.[1]

The importance attached to the role of the legislative draftsperson in the national context of promoting the rule of law and also more indirectly to ensuring that the political values cherished by the Commonwealth membership can be properly translated and reflected in a 'Commonwealth of Laws' is immeasurable. Indeed, most individuals would no doubt accept that high quality legislative drafting resources are essential to the quality of, and public confidence in, justice systems and so to the maintenance of the rule of law. Yet, despite this enormous contribution to ensuring the accurate translation of the political will of the electorate into the written word of the law, the importance attached to legislative draftspersons and to developing their craft by way of national investment, training and recognition is rarely commensurate with the real value and visibility that they amply deserve. For that reason alone, this edition which thoroughly examines the different aspects of legislative drafting is very timely indeed.

Although the Commonwealth has been engaged in the training of legislative draftspersons since 1974, the lack of a coherent strategy nationally and regionally over previous decades has led to severe capacity constraints across the Commonwealth membership which has been felt particularly acutely in smaller jurisdictions as a result of a continued shortage of qualified draftspersons. This shortage was recognised at the Commonwealth Law Ministers meeting and meeting of the Senior Officials of Law Ministries held in Edinburgh in 2008. The respective meetings

[1]A Smith, *Stitches in Time: The Commonwealth in World Politics* (Andre Deutsch Limited, Ontario 1981) 120–21.

highlighted the challenges of ensuring an adequate number of trained legislative draftspersons against the bleak reality of not enough lawyers being trained to replace those drafters leaving the field, under-resourced offices, poor remuneration and other terms and conditions of service; isolation in the performance of their work and being overworked as they are required to multi-task and carry out duties other than drafting, together with the lack of awareness among law graduates of legislative drafting as a viable career option.

The Edinburgh meeting also heard about the nature and extent of the Commonwealth Secretariat's strenuous efforts to build national capacity, provide technical assistance and to fill gaps in support of legislative drafting.

The approved work by Law Ministers of the Commonwealth Secretariat's work in this field over the past many years of its engagement is very impressive, with hundreds of individuals trained; short drafting courses developed on a regional basis, together with funding by the Commonwealth Fund for Technical Assistance (CFTC) to provide long term experts in legislative drafting of one to four years' tenure who are placed in the drafting offices of some Member States. However, despite these ongoing initiatives and a growing amount of funding being allocated in response to the increased mandates and requests received from countries for assistance, the current position as highlighted at the Edinburgh meeting is one of a perennial shortage, with problems in recruitment and retention of legal drafters. Law Ministers also recognised that it was not enough to focus on training alone as the problem required a more sustainable approach based on the adoption of different strategies under broad headings which included institutional strengthening, recruitment and retention of drafters and capacity building.

However, Law Ministers recognised that implementation of these strategies depended on the legal and administrative circumstances and priorities of each Member State. Given this scenario it is clear that Secretariat engagement in filling the 'gaps' in legislative drafting across the Commonwealth membership will need to continue for the foreseeable future; this being said, however, and mindful of the revised focus away from the provision of ad hoc technical assistance and training alone to developing and implementing sustainable strategies aimed at building institutional and technical capacity, the Secretariat itself is currently looking at how it can more closely align its limited resources to work more effectively with the needs of its membership to ensure a timely and sustainable fulfilment of these highly desirable goals which must be in the interests of all stakeholders.

Akbar Khan
Director, Legal and Constitutional Affairs Division
London, 7 December 2009

Articles

The ethics of legislative drafting

VCRAC Crabbe

Professor of Legislative Drafting and Commissioner, Statute Law Revision of Ghana

The article outlines the qualities required of Parliamentary Counsel. It notes that drafting is an extremely onerous, exacting and highly-skilled task. What is clearly conceived in the mind may not be easily expressed with clarity and precision in words. Drafters are wordsmiths, and good policy may become a bad law as a result of the bad arrangement of words in a legislative sentence – creating an ambiguity, a vagueness, an obscurity, or even an absurdity. The author notes that Parliamentary Counsel must have a strong interest in substantive policy. Yet the classic theory is that Parliamentary Counsel do not initiate policy. They are only technicians whose function it is to translate policy into law. The author concludes that legislative drafting requires the cultivation of detachment as a necessary qualification. Legislative drafting cannot hold its audience captive. It can consistently captivate its audience to the ideals behind the policy decisions that motivate legislation. In these lie its purpose, its strengths, and its value.

Introduction

May I ask you to take a walk in the garden. There you will find the flowers, the shrubs, the herbs, the butterflies and the birds. The grass looks green and fresh. The dew has done its work. All is serene, green and peaceful with the medley of colours of the flowers. Or take a walk in the forest. The big trees, the varieties of plants and shrubs. Here also you hear the twittering of the birds, the croaking of the frogs near a little stream. The rays of the sun filter through the leaves. Each little leaf gets its portion of the rays of sunshine and builds up its share of chlorophyll.

You do not see the earthworms. The earthworms. Yes, the annelid worms, living in the ground. The oligochaetes of the species play a very important role as the humus-builders in our gardens and forests. They burrow into and turn over the soil thus supplying oxygen to it which helps in the formation of the nutrients required in the soil, contributing to the improvement of the soil and the life of the garden and the forest. And, by extension, the lives of other members of the animal kingdom.

Yet they may not even be conscious of the magnitude of their achievements. That is the stuff of which Parliamentary Counsel[1] are made. That is the spirit which animates them in their daily run of things as king pins in the science of government.

---

[1] I prefer this term to the use of the word 'drafter'. 'Legislative Counsel' is another term which I prefer. At least a spelling mistake will not make those who draft legislation 'drifters'!

The legal practitioners try to understand legislation. Some even try to misunderstand what an Act of Parliament says – or the conduct required under a set of Regulations. They are those who participate in litigation. Yet other kinds of lawyers are called upon to take other legal tasks – those called upon to prepare definitive legal instruments, those who are called upon to deal with the complexities of modern life, the factual contingencies which have led to the increase in legislation.

As Reed Dickerson put it,

> the need for specialists in drafting derives from the almost inevitable complexity of the subject matter, especially when the instrument must be integrated into a system of instruments: the financial, social or political importance of the subject matter; and the not always visible inadequacy of most lawyers as draftsmen. Superior drafting requires a special kind of temperament and, even among many lawyers who have it, there is a general lack of training.[2]

Much then depends on training. The most advanced form of training is the time-honoured system of apprenticeship. It allows for guidance and advice – learning by doing has never been surpassed in any discipline. 'Theory is apt to get the cart before the horse.'[3] Yet the mind could not achieve some, at least, of its purposes but for the means to put practice into effect. Our experiences are but the effect of thinking, seeing and doing things. Practice makes perfect. That is an old adage. And practice under guidance is the most effective way to learn an art or a science. History attests to the importance of acquiring a skill by means of training. Barristers have been apprenticed to the law since the twelfth century – the genesis of what we now call pupillage.

In the field of legislative drafting, the drawback to the apprenticeship system is the lack of competent Parliamentary Counsel, especially, in young Commonwealth countries, who would supervise the training and education of aspiring drafters. Some other form of assistance is called for if we are to scratch the surface of the need for more trained Parliamentary Counsel. That calls for classroom teaching of legislative drafting, but that cannot be a substitute for the time-honoured system of apprenticeship. Distance learning can be called in aid. Yet distance learning can only be effective if there are experienced Parliamentary Counsel who will be willing to supervise the work of the distance learning student. Without that supervision, distance learning in our case is of little value. The value of the experienced hand cannot be over-emphasized.

Since 1974, the Commonwealth Secretariat has been most helpful in facilitating this task. The Commonwealth Secretariat, with financial assistance from the Commonwealth Fund for Technical Co-operation, has been organizing training courses to establish a core of well trained Parliamentary Counsel to serve as the teachers of the neophytes in their respective jurisdictions. These courses range from Crash Programmes, Short Courses, Certificate Courses in Legislative Drafting, organized in collaboration with the respective Governments, and with the University of the West Indies, the Advanced Diploma in Legislative Drafting and the LLM in Legislative Drafting.

---

[2]Reed Dickerson, 'Now that you are in it, what will you get out of it' (1960) 4 *Student Lawyer* 18.

[3]Oliver Wendell Holmes, 'The Path of the Law' (1897) 10 Harvard Law Review 457.

The qualities

Legislative drafting is a difficult task. It is an extremely onerous, exacting and highly-skilled task. What is clearly conceived in the mind may not be easily expressed with clarity and precision in words. Where something can be easily expressed, it may not be easy to do so in a way devoid of misunderstanding. It is not a task 'for children, amateurs and dabblers. It is a highly technical discipline, the most vigorous form of writing outside of mathematics. Few lawyers have the *special* combination of skills, aptitudes and temperament necessary for a competent draftsman'.[4]

Legislative drafting demands hours of concentrated intellectual labour. It is a discipline in itself. Its practitioners must have a facility in the use of the language of legislative instruments. Experience in legal practice is desirable. So is an interest in drafting, a mastery of the use of the relevant language, a systematic mind and orderliness in the formulation of thoughts, the ability to pay meticulous attention to detail and to work with accuracy under pressure.

It nurtures natural abilities of clear, cogent, concise thinking into a habit of restrained writing. Thus an enquiring, inquiring, critical and imaginative mind is a *sine qua non*. There must be the ability to work with colleagues and those skilled in other disciplines, and one must be disposed to give and take constructive criticism and advice. Common sense, economic, political and social awareness are essential. To these we must add a sense of humour.

Accuracy and precision of language may proceed from an innate habit of mind. Yet they can be acquired in many ways. Parliamentary Counsel must cultivate an attitude of rigid self-criticism. For what seems perfectly clear to them may not be equally clear to the person who reads a piece of legislation – be that person a judge, a lawyer, a law professor or what is often described as a layman.

Then there is the fallibility of human foresight and, indeed, of language itself. Yet the task of Parliamentary Counsel requires that any doubt, ambiguity, or vagueness is reduced to a workable minimum through an intelligent application of knowledge and experience. The measure of the draft's success is the ability to leave little room for doubt and ambiguity, whether semantic, syntactic or contextual.

The perfect Bill, according to Driedger, has never been drafted. It never will be.[5] Parliamentary Counsel must combine in their natures the aloofness of the Bench, the professional skills of the practising lawyer, the characteristics of the legal scholar and all the attributes of the law teacher. Indeed, it is wrong to suppose,

> that the rules of good drafting are simply the rules of literacy composition, as applied to cases where precision of language is required, and that accordingly, anyone who is competent to draw in apt and precise terms a conveyance, a commercial contract, or a pleading, is competent to draw an Act of Parliament.[6]

---

[4]Reed Dickerson, *Legislative Drafting* (Little, Brown and Co, Boston 1954) 3. And Sir Granville Ram, a former First Parliamentary Counsel at Westminster in the United Kingdom, stated that, 'only men and women of first class ability can do the work', (1951) NS *Journal of the Society of Public Teachers of Law* 444.

[5]EA Driedger, *The Composition of Legislation* (E. Cloutier, Ottawa 1957) xx.

[6]C Ilbert, *The Mechanics of Law Making* (University of Colombia Press, New York 1918) 109.

There is more to it than it is often thought or spoken of. To adapt Hart and Sacks, a Parliamentary Counsel must be

> an architect of social structures, an expert in the design of framework of collaboration for all kinds of purposes, a specialist in the high art of speaking to the future, knowing when and how to try and bind it and when not to try at all.[7]

For, 'the number of contingencies a lawyer has to guard against in the case of a will or contract, while sometimes they are numerous, are mere fly-specks compared with the contingencies that must be considered in the case of a statute.'[8]

When the wisdom of the politician fails and economic, political and social problems are at hand, when the administrator's wits are at an end and his mental fuse burns out, when the tyres of the social reformer blow out, legislation then becomes immanent and Parliamentary Counsel are called upon for their skills of drafting to sort out the myriad complexities of human frailty. Thankfully, they do not waste their sweetness on the desert air.[9]

Words

Counsellor Pleydell in Walter Scott's *Guy Mannering* was showing Colonel Mannering round his chambers, in High Street, Edinburgh. Pointing to the books on the shelves he said, 'These are the tools of my trade. A lawyer without history or literature is a mechanic, a mere working mason; if he possesses some knowledge of these he may venture to call himself an architect.'

But words are the backbone of books and of literature, and of history which for now, cannot be written but for words. They are the basic units of expression, the essential elements of a sentence to convey an idea. That idea may be a command to do a positive act or a prohibition to refrain from doing something. That places a very serious obligation on Parliamentary Counsel to use proper words and arrange the words in a manner that makes the legislative sentence clear, precise and unambiguous.

Here we recall the injunction of Jesus Christ: 'But I say unto you, that every idle word that men shall speak, they shall give an account thereof in the day of judgement. For by thy words thou shall be justified, and by thy words thou shall be condemned.'[10] Many an accused person has been found guilty as a result of the accused's own evidence.

And a good policy may become a bad law as a result of the bad arrangement of words in a legislative sentence – creating an ambiguity, a vagueness, an obscurity, even an absurdity. The appointment of the Renton Committee was an indication of how Acts of Parliament and subsidiary legislation are seen by others. The message is that Parliamentary Counsel have a duty to make the message clear, cogent and concise.

---

[7]HM Hart, JR. and AM Sacks, *The Legal Process: Basic Problems in the Making and Application of Law* (Cambridge 1958) 200.
[8]M Beaman, *Hearings before the Joint Committee in the Organization of Congress*, quoted by Reed Dickerson in 'How to write a Law', 31 (1955) Notre Dame Lawyer 5.
[9]Adapted from Thomas Gray's *Elegy in a Country Churchyard.*
[10]Mathew 12: 36.

But deliberate ambiguity may have its uses. It 'is a device for delegating authority to administrators and judges'.[11] If logically and correctly used it may lead to the development of the jurisprudence of a jurisdiction. The law is not static, nor must we aim at finality. Progress is the realization of utopias. 'The merit of deliberate ambiguity is that it *can* always be debated and voted on in the legislature. Its exploitation is thus subject to checks other than ethical.'[12]

Indeed, 'When Gotama insisted on Right Speech, when Jesus stressed the significance of every idle word, they are not lecturing on the theory of semiosis; they were inculcating the practice of the highest virtues.'[13] That is a clear warning to Parliamentary Counsel in the use of words. By the words they use, they may corrupt those in power. By the words they use, they may bring distress or deprivation to their fellow men and women.

However, a word 'is not a crystal, transparent and unchanged. It is the skin of a living thought and may vary greatly in colour and content according to the circumstances and the time in which it is used.'[14] This emphasizes the fact that 'few words have the precision of mathematical symbols.'[15] Which echoes the warning of Justice Holmes that, 'ideas are not often hard but words are the devil.'[16]

The choice of words is thus an important matter in legislative drafting. 'Needless verbosity is the mother of difficulty.'[17] It is the enemy of clarity. In a legislative sentence, it is an abomination. Proper words in proper places make the true definition of style. Words in their proper order are the significant materials of the law. Or as *Hamlet* would put it, 'Suit the action to the word, the word to the action; with this special observance, that you over step not the modesty of nature.'[18] Thus Parliamentary Counsel must have the ability, innate or acquired, to use words appropriate to the subject matter and use language devoid of colour or ornament in order to gain clarity.

Policy

Legislation is the framework by which, the world over, governments seek to achieve their purposes. Politicians and administrators use legislation to attain their cultural, economic, political and social policies. A modern state has to legislate in order to accomplish certain political objectives and particular public policies.

The idea that legislation can be used to achieve great changes in society is very attractive to politicians. They seem to believe that anything can be achieved by legislation. To them, 'A parliament can do anything but make a man a woman, and woman a man.'[19] It is hard for them to realize that not all social ills can be cured by legislation.

---

[11]Frank Newman, *A Legal Work at Congress and the State Legislatures* (Columbia University Press, New York 1959) 75.
[12]Ibid.
[13]Aldous Huxley, *Words and their Meaning* (Ward Ritchie Press Los Angeles 1940) 35.
[14]*Towner v Elsner* [1918] US 245, US 408 or 425 per Justice Holmes.
[15]*Boyce Motor lines Inc. v United States* (1952) 342 US 337 per Justice Clark.
[16]RE Megarry, *Second Miscellany at Law* (Stevens, London 1973) 152.
[17]*Good's Case* (1627) Poph 211.
[18]Act 111 Sc 2.
[19]2nd Earl of Pembroke, quoted by the 4th Earl of Pembroke on 11 April 1648 and Harleian Miscellany (1810) 5, 113.

Centuries of social behaviour cannot be laid to rest at the stroke of a pen. Society did not start with a statute book in its hands. Legislation reflects the development of society as a whole. It is a mirror of society. Herein lies the need to guard against the consequences of misguided legislation.

Parliamentary Counsel have a vital role to play in the conception and birth of an Act of Parliament. They have the duty to express legislative policy in a language free from ambiguity. Transforming government policy into law is the prime function of Parliamentary Counsel.

In the performance of that function, the Government expects Parliamentary Counsel to ensure that the Government's policies are given legal effect, by expressing legislative intention as accurately as possible, which is capable of only one interpretation, that is, the intention of the Government.

The Government also expects that Parliamentary Counsel will ensure that the Bill as drafted is in harmony with the existing legislation as well as with the Common Law or the Customary Law. An Act of Parliament does not stand on its own. It is part of the corpus of the law. Hence the reference to it as a chapter in the Statute Book.[20] Bills as drafted must also comply with parliamentary procedure.

That brings in the question of the other audience: Parliament and the public. The expectations of Parliament with regard to a Bill require that the Bill is self-explanatory and that it is arranged in a manner that allows for orderly debate. But Parliaments pass Bills to be enacted into Acts of Parliament for the public whose affairs, approaches and aspirations will be governed by the legislation. They, too, have their expectations. They, too, expect that the Act and the subsequent subsidiary legislation are intelligible, precise and free from ambiguity.

The expectations of the public stem from the fact that there are interests other than those of the Government concerned with the quality and the vitality of legislation. The policy of a piece of legislation may have its genesis from the public through the protestations of political parties. The manifesto of a political party is an undertaking that, should the party gain political power, it would introduce legislation to give effect to the manifesto's policies and philosophies – cultural, economic, social or otherwise. Its election to office is considered an endorsement of that expectation. The public expects to see legislation that reflects the policies and philosophies it has endorsed.

Parliamentary Counsel must have a strong interest in substantive policy. Yet the classic theory is that Parliamentary Counsel do not initiate policy. They are only technicians whose function it is to translate policy into law. But, like the architect or the engineer, they must be brought into the particular problem long before the actual stage of drafting a Bill.

They must not seek to initiate policy. Policy issues are the preserves of others. But how does one translate policy without understanding that policy? Herein lies the inevitability of Parliamentary Counsel getting involved in policy considerations. The training given to Parliamentary Counsel, their vast knowledge of the existing law, their experience of the probable consequences of a piece of legislation, all these matters place them on a pedestal from which they have to be consulted on policy issues and from which they need to advise and to warn.[21]

---

[20]Particularly in the United Kingdom.
[21]Like Walter Bagehot's sovereign.

Parliamentary Counsel need not be glorified amanuenses.[22] Yet the ability to discern the thin dividing line between policy and implementation, between practice and procedure, between the motive and the motivation, between the problem and the solution of the problem make Parliamentary Counsel candidates for early participation in the policy issues that lead eventually to the drafting of legislation.

In this participation, it is important that Parliamentary Counsel do not usurp the role of a policy maker. Their interest in substantive policy is not denied. Their expertise must be conceded, but they must appreciate their own limitations, learn to submerge their own feelings and thereby act with scrupulous objectivity and integrity. They should not seek to dictate policy. Only thus can they, as seasoned legal advisers, help to shape policy. It is a sensitive relationship. Knowledge of that relationship creates a wholesome attitude to public service.

In that exercise, tact tends talent and duty demands diplomacy. Purposes are measured by philosophical pragmatism. Causes and cures are considered on the anvil of effectiveness and common sense. These are the fields open to Parliamentary Counsel to contribute in improving substantive policy. It is a broad field of morality in which the use of language carries with it moral responsibilities of great magnitude. Our failures in this regard may create problems for society as a whole. A Parliamentary Counsel 'who is deferential, decently reticent, candid, and diplomatic can make much policy'[23] as a public servant.

On the receipt of drafting instructions, Parliamentary Counsel must examine and analyze the legislative proposals. Are the proposals capable of implementation? How harmoniously will the proposed legislation fit into the scheme of existing legislation? What are the alternatives? Would an amendment be appropriate rather than a new piece of legislation? What are the legal difficulties inherent in the proposals were they to become the law?

Is there constitutional legitimacy? What are the implications in the proposals for personal rights and for vested interests? There are a whole set of questions with which Parliamentary Counsel should concern themselves. The pertinent questions raise pertinent issues. The pertinent issues raise grave questions which demand policy considerations. The resolution of the pertinent issues then involves considerations which affect the policies behind the proposals. This process leads to informed policy decisions.

Conferences with departmental officials and, with the permission of the Minister, other interested persons, will make it possible to iron out areas of difficulty. Here is the area where Parliamentary Counsel deal with the precise details of the policy behind the proposals. Here is the area where Parliamentary Counsel ensure that matters overlooked are dealt with so that the Bill, as finally drafted, does not only reflect the wishes and aspirations of the sponsors, but will also be a workable piece of legislation for the benefit of society as a whole.

Matters likely to lead to litigation are dealt with here. In *Roe v Russell*[24] there was 'a failure to provide for such obvious incidents of tenancy as death with or without a will, bankruptcy, power to assign and power to sub-let in whole or in part

---

[22]James Peacock, *Notes on Legislative Drafting* (REC Foundation Inc 1961) 17.
[23]Reed Dickerson, *The Fundamentals of Legal Drafting* (Little, Brown and Company, Boston 1980) 13.
[24][1928] 2 KB 117, [1928] All ER 262.

of the demised premises'. That led Scrutton LJ to regret that he could not order the costs of the action to be paid by the draftsmen of the Rent Restriction Acts, 1920–1939.[25]

Parliamentary Counsel thus have a duty to foresee all possible eventualities that are likely to occur. If the law is drafted to specifically exclude dogs, then cats, even tigers are not so excluded. In those circumstances, 'animal' as appropriately defined would be what is required. And what about the blind man who has to rely on a dog? These are matters for Parliamentary Counsel to fill in. Once the salient questions are asked and the relevant answers are supplied, the gaps in the broad policy will be filled. Exceptions to the general rule may be required.

In drawing up the legislative scheme for a Bill, Parliamentary Counsel may include matters that had not been foreseen at the conference table, or in the Drafting Instructions. Ideas crop up which would add to the practicability of the legislation. But then they would demand, as well, interstitial policy decisions which would require the approval of the sponsors of the Bill. Here again is an area in which Parliamentary Counsel contribute to improving substantive policy. In translating the substantive policy into a Bill additional policy matters may arise. They may not have been readily apparent before the actual drafting had begun.

The ultimate responsibility for the larger policy decisions is that of the sponsors of the Bill. Yet the success of the legislation depends on the skill and competence with which Parliamentary Counsel draft a piece of legislation. Parliamentary Counsel need to provide for sanctions, and may look at alternative provisions. Should we always provide for fine or imprisonment or both? What about non-custodial sentence? Does the approach of Parliamentary Counsel give the requisite direction in fulfilling the wishes of the sponsors? The manner in which a Bill is drafted contributes to an improvement to the substantive policy.

In other words, a failure to properly translate the substantive policy into the appropriate law may adversely affect the policy. The aspirations of the law giver in those circumstances may not have been achieved. 'The most determined will in the law giver, the most benevolent and sagacious policy, and the most happy choice and adaptation of means, may all, in the process of drawing up the law, be easily sacrificed to the incompetency of a draftsman.'[26]

Rights are generally pursued against the background of political reality. At times that raises issues of a purely political nature for Parliamentary Counsel. The resolution of the political problems requires purely political considerations rather than legal considerations. But policy makers may wish to have a legal solution to a political problem. A simple issue of a reasonable time would involve an appraisal of conditions which are economic, political or social rather than legal.

It is then a matter purely for the sponsors of the legislation to determine whether, say, 30 days forms a sufficient period within which to file nomination papers for the purposes of an election. But it is within the competence of Parliamentary Counsel to determine whether 30 days forms a sufficient period within which to bring an election petition. Counsel's knowledge of procedure – both of the civil law and of the criminal law – will be called in aid in determining the issue.

---

[25]Ibid 130.
[26]Coode, quoted by Driedger (n 5) 321.

The aspirations of a people may present acute problems which border on the ethical. A political issue of the introduction of one-party state clearly involves issues of a fundamental right. Human rights activists would argue that the step would whittle down the individual rights of freedom of speech and freedom of association. The politicians would argue on the other hand that, in order to achieve social cohesion and to build a national consciousness rather than promote ethnicity, a one-party state is desirable. How does a Parliamentary Counsel, taught to fearlessly defend human rights, deal with such serious situations which run against the grain of Counsel's training?

There comes a time when Parliamentary Counsel may have to serve – not sell – their consciences and say, 'No'. Not arrogantly, but with grave humility. Not from a pedestal of superior knowledge, but in obedience to the dictates of the realities of the day. Not as a challenge to the will of our political masters, but in response to a higher sense of public duty and a nobility of service. As in Shakespeare's *Othello*, good name must be the jewel of their souls.[27]

Thinking and writing

Legislative drafting involves an appreciation of concepts and the art of seeking and using the right words. Legislative drafting, apart from expressing legal relationships, is a form of communication. The ability to communicate depends on the ability to think. One is the essence of the other. Hence Austin's assertion that,

> what is commonly called the *technical* part of legislation, is incomparably more difficult than what may be styled the *ethical*. In other words, it is far easier to conceive justly what would be a useful law than so to construct that same law that it may accomplish the design of the law giver.[28]

Perhaps it can be argued that civilization started with the use of signs and symbols, the method by which men and women expressed their thoughts or ideas. Language has taken the place of signs and symbols – except, perhaps, in mathematics. The use of language involves thinking as the idea is first conceived and then expressed in language. So language expresses human thought and human endeavour. It reflects our very way of life. Every aspect of our lives is affected by language. Sadly, language is also a source of many a misunderstanding. When Scrutton LJ says, 'I regret that I cannot order the costs to be paid by the draftsmen of the Rent Restriction Acts',[29] it is an indication that, perhaps, Parliamentary Counsel had not made the message clear enough.

Clarity is thus an important aspect in legislative drafting. It helps to eliminate ambiguity and vagueness. The first consideration to observe is that a word does not have a *meaning* by itself. Its meaning is derived from the context in which it is used. The second consideration is that of concepts. A concept is vague if in a given context it leaves open too wide a range of borderline cases to delimit precision in

---

[27] See also p [36] and footnote [41].
[28] J Austin, *Jurisprudence*, quoted by Ilbert 'The Mecanics of Law Making' (n 6) 98.
[29] *Roe v Russell* [1928] 2KB 117, [1928] All ER 262.

that context. The expression, 'A person shall not smoke', leaves a lot of questions to be answered. Smoke *what?* And its consequences?

The third consideration is that the subjective intent of the writer or speaker must coincide with the objective meaning of the word or phrase used in its context, and be so supported by an external source such as a dictionary, reasonable interpretation or even antecedent experience. If that is not the case, then, as the expression goes, 'we are not talking the same language'.

When Jesus Christ said, 'and for this cause came I into the world, that I should bear witness unto the truth. Everyone that is of the truth heareth my voice', Pilate asked Christ, 'What is truth?'[30] This type of situation arises whenever the Courts fall on the intention of Parliament in trying to construe a provision of an Act of Parliament.

The fourth consideration is that if the subjective intent attempts to meet two objective meanings, that is to say provide a reasonable compromise, equivocation can result. Mr Lloyd George, asked by a lady what was the difference between a man and a woman replied, 'I can't conceive, I can't conceive.'

There are two meanings here:

(1) I cannot perform certain of the biological functions which are the preserve of the female.
(2) I cannot for the life of me understand why there should be a difference.

In the expression, 'An employer shall ascertain from a prospective employee whether he is a graduate', the *he* is intended to refer to the prospective employee. In the sentence structure it refers to the employer who is the subject of the sentence. This type of error is often not obvious. This is an example of what Reed Dickerson would refer to as a pronominal uncertainty.

The fifth consideration is that what may normally be omitted in some contexts may not be omitted in others in the interest of clarity.

> 'For terminating a mortgage under these conditions see Schedule C. Otherwise see Schedule B. Schedule A does not apply to termination.'

See Schedule B for what? Otherwise see Schedule B implies that Schedule B does not apply for the termination of a mortgage. However, it is specifically stated that Schedule A does not apply to termination of a mortgage. So what does Schedule B stand for?

The sixth consideration is that simplicity is not clarity nor is simplicity necessarily good sense. A law which provides that, 'When two trains approach each other at a crossing, they both shall stop, and neither shall start up until the other has gone', has as its substantive policy the avoidance of railway accidents at railway junctions.[31] As drafted, the law has frustrated the intention of the sponsors. Subsection (3) of section 8 of the Crimes (Hijacking of Aircraft) Act 1972 of Australia provided that, 'The punishment for an offence against this section is imprisonment for life.' This plain simple provision led to a plain simple question

---

[30] *John* 18:37–38. See also Bacon, Of Truth, *Essays*.
[31] Taken from Gyles Brandeth, *The Law is an Ass* (Pan Books, London 1984) 126.

in *R v Sillery*[32] does the provision impose a mandatory penalty or does it confer a discretion on the Court to impose a penalty less than life imprisonment? The trial Court and the first appellate Court held that the penalty was mandatory. The higher appellate Court held that the penalty was discretionary.

The seventh consideration is that sequence will readily imply connection. *Ejusdem generis* and *noscitur a sociis* have something to do with this. The adage 'show me your friend and I will tell you your character' applies here. The principle is that, 'where there are general words following particular and specific words, the general words must be confined to things of the same kind as those specified.'[33] Equally, 'where several words are followed by a general expression which is as much applicable to the first and other words as to the last, the expression is not limited to the last, but applies to all.'[34]

So the meaning of a word can be ascertained by reference to the meaning of words associated with that word. The expression 'Cats, dogs, sheep, goats and other animals' has two basic points of identification. Each animal is *four-footed.* Each animal is *a domestic animal.* So if the reference is to *domestic animals* then 'other animals' would include hens and turkeys which are not four-footed animals. But if we are dealing with *four-footed animals* then 'other animals' would include other four-footed animals. What other four-footed animals would be included will, all the same, be related to the type of animals the context would admit.

And lastly, the maxim *expressio unius est exclusio alterius* – the express mention of one thing implies the exclusion of another. Or put another way, *expression facit cessare tacitum.* The expression *A person shall not bring a dog into a food store* means in effect that a person can bring a cat, a monkey, perhaps even a tiger into the food store! The appropriate provision would be to use 'animal' with an appropriate definition which would shut out the animals to be excluded.

A basic rule as a guide to clarity is to express only one main thought in each sentence. Where there is a complicated piece of drafting, the device of paragraphing, correctly used, would make the meaning more precise. Compactness is essential. When the parts of a sentence are widely separated it is difficult to grasp the meaning. It may be necessary to revise the draft of a Bill many, many times. 'Pride of authorship requires patient consideration and comparison of constructive suggestions for improvement from every source.'[35]

Above all Parliamentary Counsel must appreciate that, 'if the trumpet gives an uncertain sound who shall prepare himself to battle. So likewise, ye, except ye utter by the tongue words easy to be understood how shall it be known what is spoken? For ye shall speak unto the air'[36] Or to quote Confucius, 'if language is not correct, then what is said is not what is meant; if what is said is not what is meant, then what ought to be done remains undone'.[37]

---

[32](1980) 30 ALR 563, 656, quoted by IM Turnbull in 'Problems of Legislative Drafting' (1986) Stat LR 69.
[33]*R v Edmundson* (1859) 28 LJMC 213 ATP 215.
[34]*Great Western Railway v Swindon etc. Railway* (1884) 9 App CAs 787 at 808.
[35]Editorial (1951) 27 Journal of the American Bar Association 239 quoted in Reed Dickerson's, *Materials in Legal Drafting* (West Group, St Paul, MN 1981) 131.
[36]1 Corinthians 14:8, 9.
[37]Quoted by Ernest Gowars, *The Complete Plain Words* (Pelican Books, London 1983 report) 159.

Development objectives[38]

There is the need for more and more original legislative drafting. As young countries of the Commonwealth move further and further into local solutions for the cultural, economic, political and social problems that confront them, they will move further and further away from the models of legislation fostered in these countries both before and after their independence. In this regard their legislative drafting services would have to be prepared to rely more on their own resources than had been the case in the past.

Parliamentary Counsel in these countries must be technically, professionally and maturely equipped to respond to the new challenges that confront their respective countries. For legislative drafting is an attempt to solve a problem, be it cultural, economic, political or social through the instrumentality of legislation. There are no model problems. There can never be model solutions.[39]

Parliamentary offices must attain a reasonably high measure of technical proficiency. That means that Parliamentary Counsel should have more opportunities to specialize and to gain more legislative drafting knowledge and experience. That would lead to a greater measure of proficiency in the technical and professional features of legislative drafting. This should take account of the technological advances now available such as computer competency for legislative drafting.

Acquiring the necessary technical proficiency through specialization, is in economic terms, a cost factor of the legislative process. But it must be emphasized that the acquisition of the requisite technical and professional proficiency does not depend on the mere addition of legal officers to the legal staff. It also demands acquiring from within the local community the technical experts necessary for the legislative process.

Outputs and activities

The objectives to be achieved are immediate as well as long term. They are direct as well as indirect. The direct and immediate objectives are related to the continuation of the training of a core of Parliamentary Counsel. They would form the cadre for the progressive development of legislative drafting techniques in their respective countries.

The skills to be acquired in response to this relate, primarily, to three functions of Parliamentary Counsel: the amanuensis function, the professional function, and the composer function. Under the amanuensis function, Counsel learns to appreciate the limitations on Counsel's responsibilities. Policy decisions are for the policy makers. Parliamentary Counsel should not dictate policy. They should not distort policy. They should not divert policy. Their responsibility in this regard is to comprehend the policy and translate the policy into legislative form.

---

[38]What follows is a revised version of part of an article by the present author published in (1998) 19(2) Statute Law Review (Oxford University Press).

[39]A competent Parliamentary Counsel does not need a model law. The need is to draft the Bill to solve the problem at hand which may be cultural, economic, political, social or otherwise, not by reliance on models which turn out on proper examination, to be intended for other situations not germane to those at hand.

The task here is to appreciate the thin line that divides legal assistance from officious meddling. Parliamentary Counsel must learn to curb enthusiasm, dampen personal importance, and reach for an understanding of the policy issues involved in a given proposal for legislation. Here tact will tend talent, duty will demand diplomacy. These are qualities which Parliamentary Counsel must imbibe if they are ever to approach the status where they are described as competent.

Policy issues are often not clear, however much they pretend, even to the administrators. Thus Parliamentary Counsel must learn to distil from the mass of verbiage the problems that call for legislation, to foresee the pitfalls in the policy proposals, and thus be able to bring difficulties legally and administratively to the attention of the policy makers. They should present the relevant choices that sooner or later those responsible for policy must make. But, Counsel must bear in mind that,

> There are often good reasons, political or tactical, sometimes more easily appreciated by the politician than the lawyer, but in many cases very sound and cogent, against the adoption of counsels of perfection urged, and properly urged, by the draftsman from the legal point of view.[40]

Under the professional function, Parliamentary Counsel must anticipate the legal difficulties and the pitfalls, the inadequacies in the policy, and the relationship of the policy to the existing body of the law. This function permeates – and supplements – the amanuensis and the composer functions. The danger here, as far as the professional function is concerned, is that time is often the enemy. In seeking to attain perfection in their work, Parliamentary Counsel have to learn to work under pressure and even under trying conditions.

The composer function is the test of Parliamentary Counsel's competency. That test is the ability to communicate the law to the audience, that is to say, to the policy makers, to Parliament, to the prudent man of the law, to the reasonable man of the law whose life is affected by the law, and finally to the Courts. There is a difference between a legal mechanic and a legal craftsman which turns largely on an awareness of social structures, the design of frameworks of collaboration for all kinds of purposes, a specialization in the high art of speaking to the future, knowing when and how to try and bind, and how not to try at all.

The long-term and indirect objectives relate to the law-making element, the interpretation element and the communication element. The law-making element requires of Parliamentary Counsel the ability to identify the authority that has the requisite competency to instruct on policy matters. This is done in order to identify the interests concerned and thus assure the clearest and most complete line of communication. Counsel must of necessity deal with the Cabinet, the Cabinet Committee on Legislation, Ministers of the Government, civil servants, public servants and a whole body of pressure groups who seek to use the machinery of the state in order to achieve a personal or a particular political purpose.

The interpretation element has two aspects: legal and political. The political aspect of a proposed piece of legislation could provoke debate, controversy and political passion sometimes bordering on the fanatic. Parliamentary Counsel deal

---

[40]Ilbert (n 6) 18–19.

with those matters from a distance – at arm's length. Awareness of this is essential, if only because it leads to the legal effects of a proposed measure. There is obviously an overlap here. A Parliamentary Counsel is essentially a lawyer first, and Parliamentary Counsel second. There are preliminary questions of a purely legal nature that must be answered. Would the proposed measure be unconstitutional? If constitutional, what problems of fundamental human rights are involved? What would be the harmonious relationship of the proposed legislation with the existing body of law? What values of the society would be at stake?

It is under the communication element that the incompetency of Parliamentary Counsel would sacrifice the intention of the law giver. It is an important element in the legislative drafting process. Language is the vehicle of the law. It is the medium of communication. A command of the language of the law is essential. A command of the language to express the law becomes absolutely essential. It is not just a question of style and legal language. It is a question of the ability to be clear and concise, concrete and cogent. Without the ability to communicate, and communicate effectively, the whole edifice cracks. It will eventually tumble to the ground. The relevant legislation will face a very unwelcome reception by its audience.

In conclusion

In essence legislative drafting should be likened unto a focus, a stream of technical knowledge of a special kind that unites the interplay of many minds to produce a unity of thought enunciated as a command – a law that has a beneficial effect for the audiences that are subject to the law's demands. It requires the cultivation of detachment as a necessary qualification. Legislative drafting cannot hold its audience captive. It can consistently captivate its audience to the ideals behind the policy decisions that motivate legislation. In these lie its purpose, its strengths and its value.

Acknowledgements

The author is grateful to his colleagues, Mrs. Sabina Ofori-Boateng, Consultant on Legislative Drafting to the Parliament of Ghana, to Mr. Henry Tackie, Principal State Attorney and to Ms. Agnes Naa Kwarley Quartey-Papafio – State Attorney both in the Legislative Drafting Division of the Attorney-General's Office for their very valuable suggestions.

Notes on contributor

VCRAC Crabbe is an expert in the field of legislative drafting and has held a number of high-profile positions, including: Commissioner (Statute Law Revision of Ghana); Professor of Legislative Drafting (University of the West Indies, Cave Hill Campus, Barbados); Director, Commonwealth Secretariat Scheme for Legislative Draftsmen (for the West Africa, East Africa, Southern and Central Africa Regions and the Caribbean Region); First Parliamentary Counsel and Constitutional Adviser (to the Ugandan Government); Chairman (Constituent Assembly for the drafting of the 1979 Constitution for Ghana); Judge (Supreme Court of Ghana) and Senior Instructor (International Law Development Centre, Rome, Italy).

Training of Legislative Counsel: learning to draft without Nellie

Sandra C. Markman

Consultant Parliamentary Counsel, currently with the Attorney General's Office, Dublin, Ireland

There is a worldwide shortage of legislative drafters, while the volume and complexity of government legislative programmes is everywhere on the rise. Improving the efficiency and effectiveness of training for legislative counsel must be an important part of the response to this imbalance in an area crucial to good governance. In the conventional view of legislative drafting, the knowledge and skills required by drafters are often narrowly conceived and training is treated primarily as a matter of acquiring experience on the job by observing how senior drafters worked – 'sitting with Nellie'. The author believes that the conventional view underestimates both (i) the scope of the knowledge and skills that are required in the drafting activity; and (ii) the range of techniques that can be used to teach and learn the required knowledge and skills.

Introduction

For some years, there has been a worldwide shortage of legislative drafters, as the Commonwealth Law Ministers noted after their 2008 Edinburgh meeting:

> LEGISLATIVE DRAFTING
>
> 10. Law Ministers considered the perennial problem of the shortage, recruitment and retention of legal drafters and acknowledged that it was not enough to focus on training alone. This problem required a more sustainable approach based on the adoption of different strategies under broad headings which included: institutional strengthening, recruitment and retention of drafters and capacity building.[1]

The Law Ministers were certainly correct to say that training is not a complete solution to this problem, but it can be a much greater part of the answer than some might think. The good news is that increasing the effectiveness and efficiency of

---

[1]*Communiqué*, Meeting of Commonwealth Law Ministers, Edinburgh, 7–10 July 2008, p 2, para 10 <http://www.thecommonwealth.org/document/181889/34293/35232/181429/clmm2008.htm> (all websites referenced in these notes were last accessed 15 October 2009). From June 2008 to July 2009, my own very informal survey turned up advertised vacancies in Afghanistan, Anguilla, Antigua, Bermuda, British Virgin Islands, Cayman Islands, Channel Islands, Cook Islands, Democratic Republic of Congo, Falkland Islands, Hong Kong, Kosovo, Indonesia, Ireland, Kenya, Montserrat, Northern Ireland, Northern Territory (Australia), Nunavut, Queensland, Victoria and Western Australia.

drafter training does not necessarily mean spending more time and money on complex training programmes. The (not really so very) bad news is that making these improvements may require drafting offices to shed some traditional ideas on what a good training programme looks like.

The false conflict of classroom seat and shop room floor

At one end of the spectrum of possible training formats is the instructor-driven delivery of theoretical knowledge typified by the lecture system that still forms the bulk of teaching at universities and many professional schools. Here, instructors deliver synopses of key principles in a field of study and test the student's recall and understanding of these principles in a formal assessment process. A student who successfully passes through this process is deemed to be 'qualified' and therefore capable of applying these principles to solve problems in the field.

At the other extreme is the purely observational apprenticeship. The learning activity is simply sitting with an experienced worker and watching how that worker performs tasks. There is no theoretical instruction in this system, and the only assessment is the pass/fail test of whether the student can perform the tasks to the required level at the end of the training period. If so, the student has a job. If not, another name is added to the unemployment roll.

> There is an old saying in the world of people development,[2] that originated in the manufacturing industry. 'Sitting next to Nellie' was, and still is, seen by many as the most effective way of training or upskilling, as the cool kids say, someone new to a role. The idea was, one would sit alongside the most experienced member of the team (take a bow Nellie) and simply observe. After a couple of weeks of watching and mimicking, they were ready to join the production line.[3]

In the twenty-first century, it is rare to find any institution or profession that still operates at either extreme of the instructional spectrum. Most professionals not only complete some formal theoretical instruction (law school, medical school) but also participate in some period of apprenticeship (articling or 'devilling' for lawyers, internship for doctors). Nonetheless, the view that it is useless, or even counter-productive, to teach complex professional job skills through any method but 'sitting with Nellie' has a powerful persistence.

In the drafting world, it is almost an article of faith that it takes years of on-the-job experience to become a drafter capable of handling significant challenges,[4] and that virtually nothing can replace that experience or otherwise hasten a drafter's progress toward competence.[5] That perspective might not surprise those who see lawyering and legislative drafting as archetypes of conservative, hidebound,

---

[2]The comma is in the original.

[3]<http://360.jackmorton.com/2009/04/sitting_next_to_nellie.html>.

[4]The estimates usually fall between 5 and 10 years. G Bowman, 'Why is there a Parliamentary Counsel Office?' (2005) 26(2) Statute Law Review 69 at 72: '[I]t takes at least seven years to train a drafter.'

[5]Even those who see the possibility of broadening the range of training techniques often advance the notion with some diffidence. EJ Donelan, 'The Role of the Parliamentary Draftsman in the Preparation of Legislation in Ireland' [1992] 14 DULJ 89 at 90: '[T]he "sitting with Nelly" practice ... arguably could be supplemented by a more structured training with lectures and practical case work so as to reduce the period of training.'

professions. However, the relative merits of theoretical learning and on-the-job experience is a hot-button issue even in the highly innovative world of information technology.[6]

Happily, in the drafting world the dichotomy of classroom seat *versus* shop floor truly is a false one, arising in part from a failure to appreciate fully:

(1) the rich diversity of learning and teaching methods that lie between the two extremes of the training spectrum; and
(2) the very broad range of skills that an accomplished legislative drafter requires.

What does Nellie actually do?

I have created an outline of what I consider to be the basic knowledge and skills needed by a fully competent drafter (see Annex). It is based on 25 years of work in the field, supplemented by discussions with other professionals and a review of advertisements and job descriptions for legislative counsel over the past few years.[7]

This outline is intended to serve as a starting point for thought and discussion, not as a conclusive template. There is never a 'one-size-fits-all' solution to professional training. Drafting offices should add or remove elements to reflect their unique situations. The point is not that this is *the* outline, but rather that every drafting office can (indeed must) develop its own outline, and then tailor training programmes to it. No useful training programme can emerge unless those in charge of it have at least some idea of what skills and knowledge they are training towards.

What legal and practical knowledge do drafters need?

A. Legal knowledge

1. General legal knowledge

Every draft legislative instrument contains, in effect, the drafter's implicit legal opinion of its validity and effectiveness under the law of its jurisdiction.

To know what constitutes valid legislation, drafters must have a profound knowledge of their jurisdiction's constitutional and administrative law. To know what constitutes effective legislation – that is to say, legislation that faithfully translates the government's policy into legally enforceable rules – drafters must have an equally deep knowledge of their jurisdiction's statute book and of the substantive law context in which the proposed legislation will operate.[8]

---

[6] A lively online discussion was recently sparked by a suggestion that those who believe there is nothing to be learned in the classroom are missing the point. You can follow the discussion at <http://blogs.computerworld.com/node/4290#comment>.

[7] A quick Google search of terms such as 'Parliamentary counsel job' or 'legislative counsel job' will allow the reader to replicate my entirely unscientific research.

[8] Indeed, in some jurisdictions, for some fields, the drafters are required to be subject-matter experts in the area in which they draft. In the Legislative Services Branch of the Department of Justice Canada, for example, there are specialist drafting groups for the Departments of Transport, Environment and Health <http://sage-geds.tpsgc-pwgsc.gc.ca/cgi-bin/direct500/eng/XEou%3dDASG-GSRC%2cou%3d LSB-DSL %2cou%3dJUS-JUS%2co%3dGC%2cc%3dCA>.

Like every other lawyer in our regulated modern societies, a drafter must also be intimately familiar with the law of statutory interpretation (sometimes referred to as the 'canons of construction').

This general legal knowledge is what all lawyers must have if they are to do their jobs. True, drafters may need to know some parts of this law better than some of their colleagues elsewhere in government or in the private sector, but all these areas of law are taught in the law schools or bar admissions courses to all practitioners. Beyond this, however, is a specialised body of knowledge that is both unique and crucial to the legislative drafting task.

2. Specialist legal knowledge

(a) Legislative process. Even when the legislature in a jurisdiction has legal officers, governments often rely on the drafters to advise on Parliamentary law and procedure. Frequently, the drafter is the only person in the drafting project team to know the standing orders of the legislature and how they have been interpreted, and is therefore the principal source of expertise on legislative process.

(b) Drafting conventions. This brings us to the last item in this section of the outline. The attentive reader will have noticed that only now, at the end of this list of things to know, do we finally come to the subset of legal knowledge that falls under the heading 'drafting conventions'. This is not accidental.

In the conventional conception of drafters' roles, a familiarity with drafting conventions is virtually the only sort of legal knowledge that a legislative counsel regularly applies on the job. This view is far too narrow, and fails to see the full scope of the drafting enterprise. As the outline in this paper tries to make clear, the job of a legislative counsel involves much more than simply putting other people's ideas and words into the form of legislative instruments. Therefore, although a thorough knowledge of the drafting conventions in the jurisdiction is a necessary condition for effective drafting, it is far from being a sufficient one.

B. Practical knowledge

(a) Government policy. The humble people who labour for governments, rather than form them, sometimes find themselves wondering, in their idle moments, if those who provide drafting instructions see coherence in the implementation of government policy as one of the goals of good government, or as one of the obstacles to it. In any event, if consistency and coherence are ever to be achieved, let alone maintained, then legislative counsel are surely the last line of defence. Legislative counsel therefore must have a sufficiently broad understanding of a Government's overall programme to advise instructing departments when proposed provisions, although entirely defensible in legal terms, do not harmonise well with other Government initiatives.

(b) Government process. Drafters are often the only people in a drafting file who have had any exposure to Cabinet and Parliamentary process and therefore are called upon to help the officials in the sponsoring ministry negotiate their way through it. Questions such as what can be proposed (practically, as opposed to

legally) as an amendment to a bill, at what stage, and who ought to be consulted to avoid an administrative hold-up at a later stage are just a few of the practical aspects of the law-making process that Parliamentary counsel need to know.

(c) Instrument choice. A drafter's expertise should also extend to questions of instrument choice – whether a law is required, what types of provisions go into primary legislation, what goes into delegated legislation and what can or should be left to non-statutory means. Although knowing what the sponsoring ministry's goals are (or what mischief the law is meant to address) is very important, the drafter must also be able to contribute to ensuring that the method chosen for achieving those goals is an effective and proportionate one. If asked to draft a hammer to kill a fly, a good Parliamentary counsel must know enough to suggest the use of a fly-swatter instead, and perhaps even make a brand recommendation.[9]

How can drafters acquire this knowledge?

Most lawyers recognise that they have a professional responsibility to know their area of law and keep up to date. The primary role of the Parliamentary Counsel office is therefore to make it easy to access legal resources and to encourage their use.

In terms of government policy and process, the drafting office can facilitate access to internal resources by compiling a list of government publications or websites on the topic. Every drafting office should have copies of the standing orders of the legislature and is likely to have standard textbooks on drafting, Parliamentary process, statutory interpretation and constitutional law.

The drafting office can also organise short talks in any of these areas by outside experts (where resources permit and the topic justifies it) or by colleagues who research and present points of interest to others.

Even more important, in some ways, is encouraging an atmosphere of informal exchanges in the office. In some places, set times for coffee beaks will bring people together. In other contexts, simply encouraging senior colleagues to follow an open door policy will pay dividends. Any approach that aligns well with the culture of the office can be beneficial, so managers should be both inventive and attentive.

What legal skills do drafters need?

1. General legal skills

(a) Analysis. There is a lingering impression (especially amongst those who instruct drafters) that drafting is essentially a mechanical process, akin to construction. The drafter simply takes the blueprint (drafting instructions) and erects the structure (statute) according to the plan.

However, as anyone who has ever tried to build a house can attest, even the mechanical process of construction is anything but mechanical. Human error being inevitable, some vital structural element always seems to have been omitted from

---

[9]There are many resources available on this topic. An introduction to the concepts is available at <http://canada.justice.gc.ca/eng/pi/rs/rep-rap/2002/rp02_10-dr02_10/toc-tdm.html>.

the plans and, when work actually starts, some unanticipated site condition always requires the original drawings to be revised.

That is why good drafters, like good construction managers, need to be able to analyse their instructions before work begins. The drafter must be able to understand what needs to be drafted, and why, well before pen is put to paper. Laws are about conferring rights, creating burdens and changing behaviour. To create effective legislation, the drafter must understand how the particular instrument fits into the legal system of the jurisdiction and what impact it will have on its area of the law and on the statute book generally.[10]

Analysis is more than simply reading or listening to gain a superficial understanding of what is being said. It means identifying the various components of the information delivered, appraising them, integrating them into their context – legal and otherwise – and interpreting them in preparation for the next steps (flagging areas where more information is required, preparing a plan for the draft, etc.).

(b) Research. In jurisdictions where drafters work alone, or are also subject-matter experts, they are inevitably called upon to contribute to the final development of the policy for the legislative instrument they are drafting. For this task, they must quickly acquire a nuanced understanding of the state of the law and the policy options available.

Even where drafters are part of a multi-disciplinary team, and are therefore able to focus more on 'pure' drafting, they still must understand the purpose of the proposed legislative instrument, familiarise themselves with the existing law in the jurisdiction, learn how similar provisions have been interpreted in that jurisdiction, discover whether other jurisdictions have similar laws (or different approaches to similar questions) and follow how the courts there have dealt with the key issues.

All of this requires legal research.

(c) Writing. Drafting is a subset of legal writing and legal writing is a subset of writing. As Elmer Driedger put it, 'There is no special language for drafters.'[11] Before one can draft well, one must be able to write well.

Some assert that clarity in drafting is paramount. Some stress accuracy. Others are content simply to see both as essential.[12] However, it is universally acknowledged that it is impossible to translate a policy intention into a legislative instrument without the ability to design a logical document and then execute that design with language that is grammatically correct and effective in communicating the intended meaning. Bad writing makes bad law, no matter how thoroughly it may follow every applicable drafting convention.

---

[10] GC Thornton, *Legislative Drafting* (4th edn Butterworths, London 1996) suggests that there are actually five stages in the drafting process: understanding, analysis, design, composition and development and, finally, scrutiny and testing.

[11] EA Driedger, *The Composition of Legislation* (2nd edn Minister of Supply and Services Canada, Ottawa 1976) at 1.

[12] J Stark, 'Should the Main Goal of Statutory Drafting Be Accuracy or Clarity' (1994) 15 SLR 207 is a good introduction to this perennial dispute.

2. Specialist legal skills

(a) Drafting. Good drafting is not just writing well – although it must begin with that – it is also writing to meet the unique technical challenge of a legislative instrument.

> [I]t is not enough to attain a degree of precision which a person reading in good faith can understand; but it is necessary to attain if possible to a degree of precision which a person reading in bad faith cannot misunderstand.[13]

A central skill for a drafter is to be able to draft in a way that is harmonious with the rest of the statute book and therefore minimise the risk of a successful challenge to legislation based on unintentional variations in word choice or structure. Drafters must therefore have a thorough understanding of how to draft within the drafting conventions of their jurisdiction so that the language chosen does not inadvertently deviate from standard practice. In some jurisdictions, there is more than one legal system or official language to take into account.[14] Familiarity with, and conscientious use of, the 'house style' of the drafting office helps minimise differences amongst the instruments drafted by various members of the drafting offices.

This practice is not simply to ensure a beautiful statute book, although that can be a happy side-effect. A different way of expressing similar ideas risks being treated by courts (encouraged by resourceful counsel) as creating a different meaning, especially in common law jurisdictions where precedent is king. As part of expressing clearly to readers (including judges) what the law is, legislative counsel must take into account not only what courts have said about similar provisions in the past, but also the reasoning that the courts have used.

This essential attention to the larger context in which the legislation will operate must, of course, be balanced by an equally rigorous attention to the detail of its language. The indispensable foundation of any good draft is an accurate and internally consistent text. In creating the text, the drafter must be able to use the stylus for detail, as well as the broad brush for effect. In reviewing the text, the drafter must be able to read with a purpose, attending acutely to every word, rather than simply gliding an eye along the surface of the paragraphs.

In the interests of harmony and accuracy, much of what any drafter does is adapt existing statutory provisions to a new context or use. However, in almost every file there comes a time when precedents will not serve, and the drafter is forced to break a new trail with a truly novel legislative scheme or provision. Here, the drafter must call upon the same sort of creative skills that are more often associated with architecture or the plastic arts. For some drafters, the anxiety of striking away from well-worn paths is an unwelcome strain. For others, the obligation to be creative is the happiest burden the profession can offer.

---

[13] *In re Castioni* [1891] Q.B. 167 per Stephen J.

[14] For examples from Hong Kong, *see* 'One Country, Two Systems' at <http://www.doj.gov.hk/eng/public/basiclaw/basic6-2.pdf>. On the origins of the bijural system in Canada (Civil Law and Common Law) and the measures that are used to ensure that the French and English versions of the laws of Canada are equivalent, *see* <http://www.justice.gc.ca/eng/pi/franc/41/2001_2002/2001_2002.pdf> and <http://www.justice.gc.ca/eng/bijurilex/tax-fisc/gaudr/fo1.html>.

How can drafters acquire these legal skills?

1. General legal skills

(a) Analysis. Analysis is required of every lawyer and law student. Drafters will therefore have had some experience (whether in briefing cases for law school studies or more advanced analysis of live legal problems) before they begin life as drafters. The head of a drafting office needs to determine if there are weaknesses in drafters' analytical skills and identify ways to improve performance.

Being able to analyse material is not a skill unique to drafters, or even to lawyers. There are materials available on analysis in various contexts, and even exercises that could be adapted to the drafting office context. One source is business school textbooks or exercises. A quick internet search can yield results and models to adopt. A useful starting point might be this example,[15] which suggests that analysis can be split into the following components:

- Looking at the facts
- Making assumptions
- Synthesising
- Testing assumptions
- Evaluating options
- Recommending action.

Using whatever approach best suits the particular drafting office, scenarios can be constructed, deconstructed and discussed by groups of drafters led by a colleague.

(b) Research. Every legal professional needs to know the paper and electronic resources that are available in the jurisdiction. Lawyers would ordinarily be expected to know these when they come into the drafting office. Drafting offices need to ensure that new drafters have access to colleagues (either formally through training sessions or informally through an open-door policy) when additional information about the particular resources available (whether publicly or in-house) is required.

(c) Writing. There are many excellent reference works and workbooks on writing, and on legal writing. There are even some available on legislative drafting.

An internet search will provide more good free resources on better writing and grammar than one could possibly consult.[16] These can provide the drafter with basic information and exercises for better writing.

2. Specialist legal skills

(a) Drafting. Drafting offices need to prepare in-house style guides, and supplement them with lectures, discussions and formal decisions on drafting questions.

---

[15] <http://writing.byu.edu/files/How%20to%20Teach%20Students%20to%20Write%20a%20Case%20Analysis.pdf>.

[16] *Eg*, <http://www.english-the-easy-way.com/>, <http://grammar.quickanddirtytips.com/>. Another favourite site is the New York Times' 'After Deadline' blog, and its quizzes, at <http://topics.blogs.nytimes.com/2008/11/03/red-pencils-ready/?scp=1&sq=after%20dead line%20quizst=cse>.

Many drafting offices are quite willing to share their style guides on request, so that even the smallest office can generally acquire some useful models to prepare their in-house document.[17] If formal training sessions are possible, they should not confine themselves to grammar and style, but should also show how to construct a text that harmonises with the body of legislative instruments in the jurisdiction.[18]

Some drafting offices enhance quality by using second readers. These may be legally trained or their expertise may lie in other areas (proofreaders, linguists).[19] Giving junior colleagues some role in that process not only adds another layer of quality control, but also obliges them to study the work of more senior colleagues in a very focused way. There is no better way to provide training for attention to detail.

If there is not enough 'live' work in second readings, then one can easily construct written exercises where there are grammatical and typographical errors, and ask colleagues to spend some time correcting them. This kind of exercise is much more effective when the correction is done using a checklist. In fact, producing a checklist for drafters can, in itself, be a useful group exercise, creating an opportunity to identify and discuss the most common sources of error. The checklist can then be inserted into a desk book or style guide and revised regularly.

Beyond specific drills, the internet offers a wealth of useful sites, some of which are not obvious sources for learning attention to detail but rather describe themselves as 'mind training' opportunities.[20]

Similarly, there is considerable material in print on enhancing creativity, mostly in the business and self-help areas.[21] If time, distance or a shortage of human and financial resources create barriers to having an expert lead a formal seminar on developing creativity, then drafters can be encouraged to engage in self-study. If some members of the office are keenly interested, they can be encouraged to do reading on the topic and share the results in an informal presentation, or by leading exercises.

What practical skills do drafters need?

(a) Listening and questioning. Drafters are commonly thought of as people who receive written instructions and then sit quietly at their desks writing legislation. Little thought is given to the oral interaction that forms part of the average

---

[17]See also para 12 of the *Communiqué* referenced at note 1, where Law Ministers received a legislative drafting manual they had commissioned.

[18]Peter Quiggin's description of the Australian Office of Parliamentary Counsel's training programme in a paper delivered at the September 2005 London meeting of the Commonwealth Association of Parliamentary Counsel (which contains modules on drafting skills), and Duncan Berry's article on training legislative drafters in the Hong Kong Department of Justice, are both available at <http://www.opc.gov.au/calc/papers.htm>.

[19]W Robinson, 'Polishing what Others have Written: the Role of the European Commission's Legal Revisers in drafting European Community Legislation' at <http://www.opc.gov.au/calc/docs/Article_Robinson_roleofECrevisers_2007.pdf> discusses the practice in the EU. For Canada, *see* I Ludchen 'Quality Assurance Processes for Bills' <http://www.opc.gov.au/calc/docs/Loophole_January2009.pdf>.

[20]*Eg*, <http://superconscious1.blogspot.com/2008/01/attention-to-detail.html>.

[21]A search for 'creative thinking' in the English books section of www.amazon.com in the autumn of 2009 yielded over 250 results.

workday. Even in the email-obsessed environment in which many people work, instructions are often issued and modified orally and drafters must be able to understand oral instructions and ask questions in a way that clarifies the legislative objectives sufficiently to produce the required text.

Drafters must ask focused, and sometimes pointed, questions so instructing officials can understand where policy refinements are required. Drafters must also learn to persist with the process, as answers come back, until the policy truly is complete and the final refinements can be made to the draft instrument.

These exchanges must be handled with some tact and empathy to ensure that those being questioned perceive the process as one directed to improving the quality of the end product, rather than as an attack on the quality of the initial policy work.

(b) Time management. Instructions to draft legislation are often a reflexive response to an urgent, complex political or social problem. This can mean that the drafting process begins before policy implications are fully thought out, and that policy goals shift during the drafting process. Drafters must therefore be able to translate novel concepts into legislative language under fierce time pressure, especially in the peak periods that are becoming a greater proportion of the legislative year. Drafting in this environment requires resilience, capacity to concentrate for sustained periods, and the ability to switch rapidly between files while remaining effective in all.

Every seasoned drafter has had days when instructions appear simultaneously in several files that had all lain dormant for weeks – all just moments before a change of Parliamentary scheduling requires the urgent drafting of committee amendments. Drafters must learn to deliver professional results without having optimal time to concentrate and reflect. They must trust their instincts, make quick decisions and distinguish 'essential' from 'nice-to-have'.

(c) Working in teams. In caricature, drafting is the epitome of the solitary occupation. The drafter receives instructions, nods sagely, departs for a secluded office, picks up a quill pen, performs the alchemy that transforms an idea into a legislative instrument and returns with a finished statute.

While it is true that drafters do need to spend some time sitting quietly in their offices while they run the government's policy intention through the filters of drafting conventions and the statute book to produce a legislative instrument, the drafting process, as a whole, is anything but a solitary one. At every stage of the process from initial instructions to final, urgent, amendments, drafters need to be supported by, and support, a team that has at least one or two instructing officers or counsel and that can, in a complex matter, be of considerable size. Depending on the file and the resources of the drafting office, team members may include politicians, senior officials, advisory counsel from the sponsoring ministry, outside counsel, subject-matter experts and even lobbyists.

In addition, for very large files, or where deadlines are tight, the drafting work itself may be shared amongst various legislative counsel, typically with a lead drafter responsible for ensuring that the final product is a coherent whole.

In short, it is very important for drafters to be effective working in teams.

Many of the teamwork skills that drafters need are common to any profession or enterprise where cooperative effort is required. However, there are aspects of the team dynamic in the drafting environment that are not entirely generic.

To begin with, there may be tremendous variations in the experience, knowledge and expertise of the team members. Sometimes, even senior decision-makers and policy advisors have had very limited involvement with the law-making process.

The drafting process can also be an unsettling one if the legislative proposals are the result of a long and strenuous period of policy development. Officials who have spent years shepherding an initiative through successive administrations are sometimes heavily invested in even the smallest details of the proposal and can perceive the most tactful suggestion for consideration of alternatives as a threat to the project.

It is also inherent in the nature of the drafting process that areas of expertise and responsibility can overlap in uncomfortable ways. The line between drafting and policy development is especially blurry. Policy experts will often embody their ideas in particular forms of words that they are loath to abandon. On the other hand, the creation of a draft is often what brings a policy issue to the surface for the first time, and drafters may not be able to confine their comments to the strictly legal and linguistic.

Sometimes, of course, friction comes not from drafters overstepping their bounds, but from their being loath to. Especially in urgent files where policy development has not kept pace, other team members can look to the drafter to make decisions on issues that to the drafter appear to be pure policy questions.

Successfully navigating through and around these obstacles requires interpersonal skills of a very high order – a combination of empathy, tact and assertiveness that is not typically recognised as part of the drafter's skill set.

(d) Using technology. Computers and related digital devices support file management, facilitate legal and linguistic research, enhance access to precedents and standard provisions, maintain and update the statute book and regulations and, through the internet, open doors to an astonishing wealth of information. In the best-resourced offices, the whole of the drafting process, from instructions to statute revision, operates in a seamless digital environment.

As the volume and complexity of legislation continue to rise faster than the number of drafters, all drafting offices are increasingly forced to rely on computer technology to meet the demands of their governments' legislative programmes. Not all drafting offices are at the same stage in the transition to a fully digital environment, but the trend line is the same all over the world.

The days of longhand drafting are gone. Being comfortable and proficient with the latest digital technology will soon be an indispensable skill for any drafter.

Younger drafters raised in environments where digital technology is as unremarkable as gravity will not find this an issue. However, those drafters who resist learning how to use digital drafting tools may find themselves increasingly marginalised as the pace of change accelerates.

(e) Conflict management. The legislative process is a rich source of conflict. Policy choices, the legal risk assessments of those choices, legislative structure, word choice, drafting style – each of these can generate strongly-held conflicting views. These conflicts are exacerbated when deadlines are short and the issues addressed by the legislation are socially or politically charged.

Persistent conflicts can seriously impede the drafting process, even if the drafter is never one of the disputing parties. Drafters must be able to facilitate the resolution of these conflicts if they are to meet their obligation to deliver legislation on time.

How can drafters acquire these practical skills?

(a) Listening and questioning. Role-playing exercises are one of the most effective ways to learn how to be an organised, succinct and effective questioner. The exercises can be short and need only two participants (although it is always useful to have someone offer a constructive critique at the end of the exercise). An 'instructing officer' delivers an initial set of instructions. A 'drafter' reflects on what is missing or problematic and then questions the 'instructing officer'.

Preparing these exercises for the participants need not take a lot of time. One has only to look at a legislative instrument and work backwards. Take the finished product and produce a complete set of accurate drafting instructions for it. (If there is a concern that the participants are familiar with the legislation, use an example from another jurisdiction.) Then introduce a few errors into the instructions for the participants to identify and eliminate (such as suggesting a 'home' for a proposed amendment in a statute where the policy does not really fit), and create some gaps that the participants will have to fill by questioning the 'instructing officer'.

A more advanced version of the role-play can simulate a meeting with multiple participants where the 'drafter' must cope with competing 'instructing officers' who talk over each other and contradict each other.

As with any role-play, it is crucial to learning that the participants respect the process. Some people find role-playing intimidating, and try to avoid that anxiety by comic 'overacting'. Modelling the exercise first with committed senior colleagues can help set the right tone.

(b) Time management. Ideally, drafters should be offered seminars with experts, supplemented with reading materials on time management and working under pressure. These issues are not unique to the drafting world, so there is no need to create specialised materials. There is a wealth of resources geared to a general public.

Where possible, drafting offices should augment these general resources with the sharing of lessons learned and brainstorming of possible solutions to real or simulated scenarios. The head of the drafting office can nominate discussion leaders to become more knowledgeable on the subject. Choosing someone who struggles in this area is sometimes an effective way to deliver maximum benefit to the person with the greatest need.

(c) Working in teams. The challenges of working in multidisciplinary teams exist in many professions.[22] Materials and courses can be acquired and adapted,[23] and

---

[22] *Eg*, <http://www.engconfintl.org/8axabstracts/Session%205B/rees08_submission_13.doc>, <http://www.hseea.ie/Performance%20Mgt/Sept%2004%20-%20Working%20in%20teams.pdf>.

[23] *Eg*, <http://www.ntc.blm.gov/leadership/employee_teams.html>, <http://www.trainersnetwork.ie/topics6.html>, <https://www.cs.tcd.ie/~smcginns/3BA6/Lectures/Working%20in%20Teams.pdf>, <http://store.teambuildinginc.com/items/shop-by-topics/team-building/list.htm>.

the head of a drafting office should encourage sharing of lessons learned and helpful techniques amongst the staff.

The need to acquire 'soft' interpersonal skills such as assertiveness and empathy is also not unique to drafters. Again, materials[24] and courses are available that can be used and adapted as required.

(d) Using technology. This is the area where it is hardest for drafting offices to find acceptable alternatives to professional training programmes. It is therefore crucial that those who manage drafting offices insist that adequately-resourced professional training is always an integral part of the implementation budget for any new technology that is introduced into the office.

Where there are weaknesses in the use of currently-installed hardware or software, informal instruction or modelling by colleagues can be of some benefit, but these techniques are very time-consuming. There are also all manner of instructional resources in print and online, but these are usually of limited value to drafters who are struggling to acquire the skills needed to access or understand them.

(e) Conflict management. This is another area where there is a wealth of resources available (written materials[25] as well as seminars and courses[26]). This is not to suggest that drafters need graduate level university training in conflict resolution,[27] but rather that an introduction to the principles of resolution of conflicts is invaluable for any drafter. If resources permit, an introductory seminar by an expert is ideal, but self-study can also be very effective, especially if followed by a discussion in the drafting office where drafters can share experiences and best practices.

In conclusion

Even if one believes that Nellie is the *best* teacher, she need not be the *only* teacher. Indeed, if drafting offices are to satisfy governments' increasing appetite for legislation, then other ways must be found to develop the skill and competence of junior drafters. There are not enough Nellies around for juniors to sit with, and those who can be found are already stretched thin by the effort to handle growing workloads.

Fortunately, once one has an appreciation for the true scope of the knowledge and skills that drafting requires, it becomes possible to create a range of rich learning opportunities to foster professional development while Nellie is busy elsewhere.

---

[24]*Eg*, <http://www.speak-first.com/news/assertiveness-skills-and-techniques-film.aspx>, <http://www.assertiveness-training.org.uk>, <http://ilearn.senecac.on.ca/careers/succeed/developing.html>.

[25]<http://www.crnhq.org/pages.php?pID=7>, <http://www.helpguide.org/mental/eq8_conflict_resolution.htm>.

[26]<http://www.businesstrainingworks.com/Negotiation-and-Finance/Conflict-Resolution-Training.html>, <http://conflictresolutiontraining.net/conflict_resolution_training/Conflict_Resolution_Training__Welcome.html>.

[27]<http://www.tcd.ie/Graduate_Studies/prospectivestudents/courses/taught/coursepg.php?course_id=43>.

Notes on contributor

Sandra C. Markman is consultant legislative drafter and trainer. For the past year, she has been in Dublin, Ireland, where she is a Consultant Parliamentary Counsel in the Attorney General's Office, drafting legislative instruments as well as developing and delivering training to drafters. A native of Montreal, Ms Markman was called to the Bar there in 1980 and then entered private practice. In 1984, she moved to Ottawa to obtain a Diploma of Legislative Drafting from the University of Ottawa. After her graduation in 1985, she joined the Department of Justice Canada, where she spent 22 years as a legislative drafter and manager. Since 2007, Ms Markman has worked as a consultant in the Caribbean and Europe.

For some years, Ms Markman served as an adjunct (part-time) professor in the Faculty of Common Law at the University of Ottawa, teaching legislative drafting and related subjects to undergraduate and graduate law students. In the 1999–2000 academic year she taught full-time as part of an exchange between the University and the Department of Justice. In 2008, she was an Instructor in the course for Parliamentary Counsel offered by the Commonwealth Secretariat in Georgetown, Guyana for Parliamentary Counsel from the Caribbean region.

Ms Markman has made presentations on drafting and legislative process issues to officials from Sweden, South Africa, Vietnam, Pakistan, Bangladesh and China. She has also served as an expert for the ILO in Geneva on the preparation of its drafting manual for international instruments.

ANNEX

LEGISLATIVE DRAFTING
KNOWLEDGE AND SKILLS OUTLINE

I. Knowledge

A. Legal

(1) *General*
- (a) Constitutional law
- (b) Administrative law
- (c) Law of statutory interpretation
- (d) Statute book
- (e) Substantive law (subject specific)

(2) *Specialist*
- (a) Legislative process
- (b) Drafting conventions

B. Practical

- (a) Government policy
- (b) Government process
- (c) Instrument choice

II. Skills

A. Legal

(1) *General*
- (a) Analysis
- (b) Research
- (c) Writing

(2) *Specialist*
- (a) Drafting

B. Practical

- (a) Listening and questioning
- (b) Time management
- (c) Working in teams
- (d) Using technology
- (e) Conflict management

Teaching legislative drafting: reflections on the Commonwealth Secretariat Short Course

Robin Webster

Former Chief Justice of Tonga, Course Director, Commonwealth Secretariat Caribbean Short Course, 2007–8

This article provides background to the Commonwealth Secretariat Caribbean Short Course in Legislative Drafting. It explains the principles on which the Course has been based and the author, the Course Director, gives some details of how it has been taught and assessed. It looks at some of the problems which have arisen and the results which have been achieved, concluding with a review of possible alternatives.

Background

For many years the best way to teach legislative drafting was thought throughout the Commonwealth to be on-the-job training over a prolonged period, and indeed that was the way I was trained myself. My own formal training in drafting years ago consisted in two UK Civil Service courses of four days each – one on statutory instruments and the other on Parliamentary Bills.

That was very much in contrast to the academic teaching at US and Canadian universities, which have for long taught drafting as an academic subject and built up expertise in doing that.

But for decades the Commonwealth has been troubled by an acute shortage of trained legislative drafters. My own view is that this is because of the nature of the job, which is only suited to certain people. The task requires precision of both mind and language, plus independence and a firmness of purpose: these are rare qualities which seldom occur simultaneously in the same person, let alone coupled with the necessary intellectual capacity and knowledge of the law. And by all standards, it is a backroom job, without any of the glamour of starring in court appearances which so appeals to young aspiring advocates in developing countries. No press headlines for the successful drafter, as for the successful advocate. Instead, if a Bill is a winner, the credit is the Minister's, whereas if it is a disaster, blame the drafter.

While much of the drafting work in post-independence Commonwealth countries has been done by expatriate drafters, it is only natural that these countries should want their own nationals to be doing their drafting. So the developing world could not wait for the 7–10 years required for training drafters on the job.

To meet that demand, two different types of course came into being. One was the university based LLM lasting up to a year, most notably from the University of the West Indies in Barbados and the Institute of Advanced Legal Studies at the

University of London; and the other was the short course of 1–3 months run by organisations such as the Royal Institute of Public Administration International in London.

However even these excellent courses were not enough to meet the demand; and most developing countries, especially small states and small islands, cannot spare key personnel, even junior lawyers, for a whole year.

The 2002 Commonwealth Law Officers' Meeting at St Vincent stated in its final communiqué:

> 31. Despite many initiatives over the years, there continue to be problems in many parts of the Commonwealth in attracting, training and retaining legal drafting staff. The quality of legislation, which often addresses matters of great complexity, suffered and law reform programmes could be delayed. The length of the existing training courses was seen as disadvantageous, and the hope was expressed that shorter courses could be arranged to supplement in-house training. The Meeting noted that the Commonwealth Secretariat was working with the Commonwealth of Learning to expand its distance learning programme and that an on-line version would soon become available.

A third way: genesis of the Short Course

The Commonwealth Secretariat's initiative with the Commonwealth of Learning, noted in that communiqué, did not come to fruition, and the Secretariat then developed a Short Course with Professor Keith Patchett. Professor Patchett based this on his own extensive experience teaching at the University of Wales in Cardiff and the Royal Institute of Public Administration International courses:

> The following curriculum is designed to provide foundation training for relatively new entrants to drafting offices that can be delivered in the equivalent of 3 months' full time study. It derives from the author's experience in organising and delivering full and part time courses of lengths varying from 6 months to 2 weeks and authoring and assessing for the Commonwealth Distance Training Course in Legislative Drafting, a joint initiative of the Commonwealth Secretariat and the Commonwealth of Learning.[1]

Following this, the Commonwealth Secretariat in November 2003 convened a workshop in Barbados of Attorneys-General and legislative counsel from the Caribbean region to make proposals for the development of a curriculum for the training of legislative drafters.

The principal aims of the workshop were to formulate for recent entrants to Government drafting offices the contents of a foundation training programme to take full account of the needs of drafters at that stage of their service and of their offices; to recommend how and by whom such a programme could most satisfactorily be instituted for the Caribbean; and to advise as to how a pilot programme might be put into effect. In their discussions the workshop also bore in mind that their work was intended to assist other regions and countries in the Commonwealth concerned with similar issues.

---

[1] A Curriculum for Training Legislative Drafting – paper presented by Professor Patchett to Barbados workshop, November 2003.

While the workshop expressed serious concern that the Caribbean region continued to be affected adversely by a shortage of lawyers interested in entering a drafting office and therefore available for training, it reaffirmed that the principal problems in the recruitment and retention of drafters lay in the terms and conditions of service and perceptions about the unattractiveness of the job among both the public and lawyers; and recognised that it was unlikely that improvements in training alone would solve these problems.

But the meeting recognised that sound training arrangements could have a beneficial effect, at least in countering the apparent unattractiveness of the work, by raising the profile of drafting as a legal activity of national importance and capable of giving considerable intellectual satisfaction, by contributing to career development and by making new and potential entrants more comfortable about the work and more committed to undertaking it.

In response to that demand, the Commonwealth Secretariat therefore began a series of what it describes as Short Courses, based on the Patchett curriculum and lasting 12 weeks, for three regions of the Commonwealth: Africa, the Caribbean and the Pacific. The curriculum for the first Course in Africa was developed in June 2005 by the Secretariat, in collaboration with legislative drafters from 18 Commonwealth African countries to reflect the realities and needs of the region. The Secretariat believed that approach to be both practical and cost-effective. It sought to provide practical assistance to Member States to help build their legislative drafting capacities and strengthen institutions for good governance.

The first African course started in January 2006, run at the University of Ghana by the indefatigable Professor Justice Vincent Crabbe.

The syllabus for these Short Courses is essentially the curriculum drawn up by Professor Patchett in 2003, but each region and Course Director has been allowed to develop it in a way appropriate for that region. For example, in the Caribbean, adaptations have been made to include the effect of CARICOM and its implementation.

The Caribbean Short Course

It was at that stage that I came in. Relaxing after a spell as Chief Justice of Tonga, I was asked to take on the task of being Course Director for the Commonwealth Secretariat Caribbean Short Course to be held at the University of Guyana in early 2007. So, equipped with the bare bones of the curriculum, I set about putting flesh on them and mapping a course covering 12 weeks, which for a full-time course devoted to one subject is indeed a very long time, despite the appellation 'Short'.

It is perhaps not well known that the famous former Secretary-General of the Commonwealth, Sir Shridath Ramphal, was once First Parliamentary Counsel in the Attorney-General's Chambers in Guyana, and there have been many other well-known drafters from Guyana, such as Professor Brynmor Pollard and Justice Duke Pollard (both of whom participated in the teaching), so it was a suitable setting for the Course.

Holding the Course at the University provided an academic setting for it and also much essential administrative back-up. The Courses were made most welcome at the Department of Law, headed by Professor Justice Aubrey Bishop.

The Course was sponsored by the Commonwealth Secretariat, in order to encourage broader participation from across the Commonwealth.

The aim of the Course was to provide an in-depth analysis of the principles underlying legislative drafting and a thorough introduction to sound drafting practice; to develop competence in the basic essentials of drafting; and to lay a solid grounding to permit useful drafting tasks to be confidently and reliably assigned to new drafters.

This is no ordinary task to carry out in 12 weeks.

Having read Professor Patchett's paper for the Barbados meeting and his subsequent report, as well as Professor Reed Dickerson's excellent discourse 'On Teaching Legal Writing, Particularly Legal Drafting',[2] it was very apparent that exercises and assignments had to be the backbone of the Course, although naturally they should follow the teaching of the principles of drafting which they exemplified. However in a tightly packed course with two major exercises per week the latter proved easier to state than to achieve.

While there are several facets to teaching drafting – putting words together, drafting procedures, and political (with a small 'p') and Parliamentary considerations – I consider that the first, putting words together, is by far the most important, because without that skill the other two facets count for almost nothing. Therefore the exercises concentrated on that skill.

Although legislative drafting demands a high degree of intelligence, it is essentially a practical subject, not an academic one, which is why predominantly on-the-job training has traditionally been used in the UK and the Commonwealth. Accordingly, in order to develop the skills, techniques and know-how that are the fundamentals of legislative drafting and basic to the actual practice of drafting, the learning focus throughout was on acquiring the *practical* skills for performing the most common and important drafting tasks, rather than covering every aspect of the theory and the drafting of all types of legislation.

I emphasised to the students that this was a professional course and that they were expected to approach it as professionals, not as students, and to conduct themselves accordingly.

Throughout the Course, the students were given two exercise assignments each week, and as the exercises became more difficult, so more time was allowed to think about them and complete them.

Course overview

I found that, in all the hustle and bustle of lectures and exercises, it was easy for the students to lose sight of the aims and modalities of the Course (*as stated above*), so to keep their focus I reminded them of these and the structure of the Course from time to time. In that way, I hoped they would continue to be able to see the wood from the trees.

The Course was divided into the following Modules:

(1) BASIC ELEMENTS of analysis, methodology, composition skills and essential knowledge of drafting processes;

---

[2]In *The Fundamentals of Legal Drafting* (2nd edn Little, Brown and Company, Boston 1986), Appendix F.

(2) EXPANDING the BASIC ELEMENTS, in particular to take in more demanding skills, drafting of particular statutory components, and to begin to take account of the constraints on drafters;
(3) APPLICATION OF MODULES 1 and 2 to new circumstances and revisiting and reinforcing factors influencing actual practice.

The Modules together contained the following Parts, which formed the basis of the Course:

(I) Introduction
(II) The drafting process
(III) Drafting constraints
(IV) The legislative process
(V) Legislative syntax
(VII) Legislative style
(VIII) Legislative structure and arrangement
(IX) Drafting preliminary and final provisions
(X) Substantive provisions
(XI) Drafting subsidiary legislation

For some reason there has never been a Part VI!

The two Courses I have run have had 13 and 12 students respectively, which is at the maximum number of 12 suggested at the 2003 Barbados workshop. For reasons outlined below I believe this is the working maximum, though I am aware of proposals to increase this number.

Instruction

Apart from the exercises, instruction was done by lectures (using PowerPoint presentations wherever possible), discussions, group discussions, drafting workshops and role plays. I have been fortunate in having a team of experienced and enthusiastic lecturers and tutors from both within and outside Guyana. Each student was given an individual tutorial and review of work at the end of each week, which I understand they valued.

Many of the students seemed surprisingly reluctant to take part in classroom discussions with the lecturer in front of the whole class, despite frequent encouragement to do so – and despite in my view having no reason to be bashful in light of the quality of their drafting work. However the position was different in group discussions, where some lively debates ensued, as also in the role plays (*see below*).

Materials

The principal textbook used for the Caribbean Course was *Legislative Drafting* by GC Thornton,[3] known to me and the other lecturers as the drafter's Bible.

---

[3](4th edn Lexis Law Publishing, Charlottesville, VA 1996).

Thornton is such a good, universal, practical book for the drafter that I was more than pleased that, thanks to a gift from the British Foreign and Commonwealth Office and the British High Commission in Georgetown, for the second year the Course was run loan copies of Thornton were given to each student. These will thus again be available to students in future years. It is difficult to describe to a non-drafter the significance of this, except to say that no drafter should be without Thornton at her or his elbow to answer any query. To my mind it is the best current drafting book: but it is also an expensive volume, so this gift was of immense help. In addition, the Commonwealth Secretariat made available presentation copies to be kept by each student who completed the Course and gained the Certificate. In this way an up-to-date copy of Thornton will be available to these students and hence to their drafting offices.

Students were given a reading list, and some of the other books were available in the University Library. The list included *The Fundamentals of Legal Drafting* by Dickerson; *Legislative Drafting* by Crabbe; and *Craies on Legislation.*[4]

As secondary sources I used *The Elements of Drafting* by Piesse; and some excellent modern books such as *Plain Language for Lawyers* by Asprey; *Legal Writing in Plain English* by Garner; *Legal, Legislative, and Rule Drafting in Plain English* by Martineau and Salerno; *Modern Legal Drafting* by Butt and Castle; and *Legislative Drafting: Principles and Techniques* by Atre and Lahoti.[5] On statutory interpretation I used Cross on *Statutory Interpretation*; and *Maxwell on Interpretation of Statutes.*[6] I also drew from a treasured volume, *In on the Act* by Sir Harold Kent, a former English Parliamentary Counsel and Treasury Solicitor.[7]

On treaties and treaty drafting the preferred text is Aust's *Modern Treaty Law and Practice.*[8]

In the second year of the Course, as each student had a personal copy of Thornton, access to other drafting textbooks was not essential. And as the Course was designed to enhance drafting skills, the need for extensive legal research, such as would normally be done by a drafter, did not arise and so a full law library was not necessary.

Participants were also asked to bring an English dictionary and thesaurus and an English style guide, such as Gowers' *Complete Plain Words* or Partridge's

---

[4]R Dickerson, *The Fundamentals of Legal Drafting* (2nd edn Little, Brown and Company, Boston 1986); VCRAC Crabbe, *Legislative Drafting* (Cavendish Publishing, London 1993); *Craies on Legislation* (2004) and its 1st Supplement (8th edn Sweet & Maxwell London 2005).

[5]EL Piesse, *The Elements of Drafting*, ed JK Aitken (9th edn Gaunt, Holmes Beach, FL 1996); M Asprey, *Plain Language for Lawyers* (3rd edn Federation Press, Annandale NSW 2003); BA Garner, *Legal Writing in Plain English* (The University of Chicago Press, Chicago 2001); RJ Martineau and MB Salerno *Legal, Legislative, and Rule Drafting in Plain English* (West, Eagan, MN 2005); P Butt and R Castle, *Modern Legal Drafting: A Guide to Using Clearer Language* (2nd edn Cambridge University Press: New York 2006); BR Atre and RC Lahoti, *Legislative Drafting: Principles and Techniques* (2nd edn Universal Law Publishing, Delhi 2006).

[6]E Cross, *Statutory Interpretation* (3rd edn Butterworths, London 1997); PStJ Langan, *Maxwell on Interpretation of Statutes* (12th edn Sweet & Maxwell, London 1969).

[7]HS Kent, *In on the Act. Memoirs of a Lawmaker* (Macmillan, London 1979).

[8]A Aust, *Modern Treaty Law and Practice* (Cambridge University Press, Cambridge 2000).

Usage & Abusage, plus their own country's Constitution and its Interpretation Act. I was quite content for the students to have an ordinary working dictionary, as if we are to draft understandable legislation we must in general confine ourselves to words in everyday use.

Teaching the essentials

During the Course, as the students were presented each day with more and more material, I found that it was important to keep reminding them of the essentials of drafting which I wished to get over to them. The following presentation and aide-memoire thus developed:

ESSENTIALS OF DRAFTING

GET IT RIGHT!
GET THE PLAN RIGHT
GET THE LEGALITIES RIGHT
GET THE WORDS RIGHT
GET THE RIGHT BALANCE

GET THE PLAN RIGHT
IE THE GENERAL SCHEME & PICTURE, ALSO THE ANALYSIS
Do you need legislation?
Montesquieu's Principles
Dickerson's Checklist
Ilbert's Questions
Thring's Rules
Legislative scheme & sequence
Statement of purpose ??

GET THE LEGALITIES RIGHT
DON'T DO ANYTHING THAT IS LEGALLY IMPROPER
Special responsibility areas
Constitutional rights & constraints
Rule of law
No retrospection
Interpretation Act
Vires of subsidiary legislation
No sub-delegation
No Henry VIII clauses

GET THE WORDS RIGHT
7 Cs
THE RIGHT WORDS
IN THE RIGHT ORDER
WITH THE RIGHT PUNCTUATION

7 Cs
Especially clarity, communication, certainty, consistency
Thornton's Rules

THE RIGHT WORDS
Rules of construction –
  Plain meaning of words in context of whole Act
Plain language

Gender neutral
Not vague/emotive/abstract
Active voice/present tense/positive
No archaisms
And/or

IN THE RIGHT ORDER
Coode's Rules
No dangling or squinting modifiers
Break it up/tabulation

WITH THE RIGHT PUNCTUATION
Thornton's Guide

GET THE RIGHT BALANCE
Not over or under
Not too general, not too specific
No obesity
Simplicity & precision
Watch definitions

While I am sure not every drafter would agree with that scenario – especially the inclusion of lists of principles and rules which some might think outdated – if all my students knew and applied, for example, Montesquieu's Principles all the time they would produce some marvellous drafts.

Drafting workshops

Focused drafting workshops evolved during the Course to help some of the students who were having trouble getting the hang of framing short legislative sentences simply.

First there was the handout to ensure all had the principles firmly in mind:

WRITING THE LEGISLATIVE SENTENCE

Decide on the SUBJECT
If imposing a duty or creating an offence, make a PERSON or ENTITY the subject
Ie the person or entity to whom a power, right or privilege is granted or on whom a duty, obligation, or prohibition is imposed
Use the SINGULAR

Then decide on the VERB
Make it STRONG, PUNCHY and POSITIVE
Use the ACTIVE VOICE
Use the FINITE VERB
Use the PRESENT TENSE and the INDICATIVE MOOD

Then think about the rest of the PREDICATE
Including MODIFIERS, CONDITIONS, EXCEPTIONS
Take care with WORD ORDER
Use PARALLEL PHRASING
TABULATE

Keep the sentence SHORT
Limit it to ONE THOUGHT

The workshop was then conducted in groups, using examples taken from recent legislation throughout the Commonwealth, so as to frame simple basic legislative sentences, such as:

Vehicle fleet emissions
It is desired to impose on vehicle manufacturers a duty that each of its vehicle fleets for a model year meets the requisite greenhouse gas emission standards.

Apology
It is desired to provide that if someone apologises, that does not amount to a legal admission of liability and cannot be led in evidence.

Exercises

I considered it important to get the class into drafting immediately at the start of the Course, so the exercises started with some redrafting of provisions from old or badly drafted statutes, which are regrettably plentiful in the statute books (eg section 89(8) of the UK Civil Defence Act 1939), then passed to drafting simple regulations (such as regulations for a straightforward government savings bank), as these are likely to be the first things young drafters are given to do. After that we moved on to exercises on grammar and syntax, plain language and writing style (strong verbs, active voice and no nominalisations). Then it was single clauses (eg giving powers to make secondary legislation), exercises on drafting instructions (for a bill to curb stray dogs) and planning a whole piece of legislation (on dealing with animal diseases). We had exercises on the important preliminary and final provisions and offence provisions, and only after these exercises were students asked to tackle drafting completely new primary legislation (in this case setting up a technical development board).

Normal procedure was to issue the exercise, possibly the previous weekend to allow time for reflection (though that risked being ahead of the teaching), then have a brief session before it was attempted, going through the exercise with an explanation of what was required. Sometimes one question was done or started as a group discussion, which was a good way to bring out the various points to be taken into consideration, as the students were more ready to take part in that, than a general discussion in the classroom. To simulate real life, I asked students to be careful to provide exactly what was asked for and to hand in exercises on time.

The students were given an appropriate time for doing the exercise, perhaps some time during the working day and almost inevitably time in the evening out of hours. The students thought they never had enough time, but that is like life in a drafting office and I insisted that exercises were handed in on time. Even if a student felt that what he or she was being asked to draft was improper or inappropriate, or that there were legal problems about anything requested, they were asked to draft the provision in any event, and if they had time, to write a letter to the Minister explaining the position – otherwise it would be a convenient way out for the idle!

As I had set the exercises several months ahead, the details were out of my mind when the exercises came to be done, so as a reality check I started attempting them myself, which helped me to gauge their level and ensure that they were suitable.

Most students did their exercises on computer, saved them on memory sticks and then had them printed out. A printed copy was certainly the preferred format for submitting exercises and I believe the few who hand-wrote their exercises put themselves at a disadvantage, both in the amount of repetitive writing they had to do and the readability of their exercises.

After I had looked through the answers I then went over the general points from the whole exercise in a further general session in class. Sometimes a suggested model solution was shown as a PowerPoint presentation. Later I marked the exercises one by one, and at the tutorials, I went over with the students individually, to discuss any particular difficulties.

On the subject of exercises I quote from Professor Reed Dickerson:[9]

> The classic method is to have the instructor or a teaching associate prepare a detailed critique of each student paper. Although this is not as effective as the idealized master–apprentice approach, the latter is beyond the practical reach of educational institutions. As the theoretically next-best alternative, personal attention to individual student papers has been routinely accepted as a sine qua non of instruction in legal writing.
>
> Wherever adopted, this assumption has effectively aborted large-class instruction in legal drafting in the law schools. Almost no senior professor will touch such a course because, in the absence of enough affordable teaching assistants, he is unwilling to suffer the numbing burden of analyzing and discussing individual student drafts, which are much more demanding than ordinary expository exercises. Putting that burden on junior instructors has failed because they are only rarely trained in the drafting discipline, and the traditional editorial tedium has resulted in high turnover. Worst of all, the intellectual challenge of most classroom writing projects (as traditionally conducted) is relatively low. This is unlikely to intrigue the better legal minds.

I echo Professor Dickerson's views that marking of drafting exercises is difficult and time-consuming, as it involves giving consideration to almost every word, particularly when endeavouring to maintain consistency and fairness. This is also a good reason for restricting the numbers on a Course.

Use of precedents

One of the problems encountered with all the exercises was the use of precedents. In reality all drafters make use of precedents, but among skilled drafters they are normally used simply as a checklist to ensure that all that needs to be covered is in the draft, or perhaps as a framework around which words appropriate to your own jurisdiction are placed. At the very minimum the precedent is properly adapted for the drafter's jurisdiction. However some of today's trainee drafters, in common it seems with some students everywhere, apparently prefer the simplicity and ease of

---

[9]R Dickerson, *The Fundamentals of Legal Drafting* (2nd edn Little, Brown and Company, Boston 1986) Appendix F – 'On teaching legal writing, particularly legal drafting'.

lifting a precedent untouched and presenting that as their solution to an exercise, saving themselves some effort, but unfortunately learning absolutely nothing about the skills of drafting.

Marking exercises

Giving marks for drafting exercises and assignments itself has its own problems. Do you simply deduct marks for each word and arrangement of words which produces the wrong result legally? Or do you give one overall mark for the style and general content of a draft? Accepting that drafting is an art rather than a science, do you reflect that by awarding marks for artful and elegant drafting? How do you mark a draft which is legally competent but drafted in a style which is the antithesis of the up-to-date best practice in drafting which you are trying to teach? I suspect that I actually use elements of all these aspects, and certainly drafting colleagues on the Course have never disagreed on how we mark particular drafts.

For exam scripts, where students are asked to draft a simple Bill without reference to anything except a dictionary or thesaurus, I have adopted a more systematic approach. I make a note of the key matters which must be covered in the Bill and award a point for each, then use these as a basis for percentage marks, with some adjustment to take account of style and how close the script is to an oven-ready Bill.

Points from exercises

Throughout the Course, there were some general points which came up time and again from the exercises. I tried to get the students to keep these constantly under review:

Failure to think through the whole draft;
Grammar – subject, verb, predicate – and remembering the verb;
Saying things negatively rather than positively;
Not breaking down the text to 1 idea per unit;
Dangling or squinting modifiers;
Not using words consistently throughout the draft;
Not considering whether all the words were needed;
Not avoiding archaisms;
Lack of consistency in using singulars and plurals.

These may not be a surprise to experienced drafters. It sometimes worries me that such elementary faults occur so frequently that it must be a criticism of the teaching, but I think in reality it is all part of the learning process.

Standards of English

One difficulty I have encountered is the variability of the standard of English, especially written English, among the students. English is the language in which they are drafting, but in reality it may not be their first language. They may have been taught it extremely well, or they may not have been taught it well at all, I have found considerable discrepancies within a region or even within a country. But it must be very difficult for those who have not been taught English well to struggle to draft with precision in a language of which they are not master. So when teaching syntax and style, the instructor has to remember that points of grammar, which come naturally to him or her, may need to be taught carefully and the nuances of language emphasised.

Tutorials

As Course Director, I gave each student an individual tutorial each week (or every second week when sharing the burden with a colleague). This took the form of individually going through each student's exercises for that week, but students were free to raise other subjects, and did so. Sometimes an entire day could be occupied by this process, as in a drafting exercise every sentence and almost every word has to be considered so that students can gain maximum benefit. I found this and (as already mentioned) the marking of the exercises, a considerable and time-consuming task, though it was made worthwhile by the consistent high standard of some of the exercises.

Role plays

To provide some variety, three role plays were carried out, the first on Parliamentary scrutiny of a statutory instrument; and the second and third on conferences with civil servants to discuss drafting instructions. In each case the material chosen for the role play was an exercise which the class was undertaking at the time. Roles were assigned in advance and the actors mostly did their homework well, so that there were lively sessions.

I found these role plays were successful in injecting some colour into what can be a drab subject; and in bringing out vividly the areas of difficulty in legislating and the types of conflict which arise in these situations. It also encouraged students to be able to hold their own in oral presentations, so that if they are called to appear before Select Committees of Parliament as drafters they are properly able to answer questions and present issues on their legislation.

Constitutions and Interpretation Acts

Two separate sessions were carried out, with the purpose of encouraging students to study their own country's Constitution and Interpretation Act. They were each asked to speak to the class for three minutes on an aspect or aspects of their own Constitution, and separately their own Interpretation Act. Where there was more than one student from a country, they were given in advance a list of possible topics for each session, which they divided amongst themselves. In this format we managed to avoid too much repetition and also to elicit some interesting information for the Course as a whole on the differences between countries, most of which began with a Westminster-type Constitution. Indeed, on one course, the session on Constitutions was one of the highlights.

Outside visits

To provide some further leaven and endeavour to show drafting in action (if that is not a complete impossibility) outside visits were made to the drafting section of the

Attorney-General's Chambers in Georgetown, Guyana and to the drafting section of the CARICOM Secretariat Headquarters, also based in Georgetown, as well as the National Assembly of Guyana.

Regional specialities

Also, by universal request, much regional material on treaties and drafting has been incorporated in the light of the CARICOM regime, eg introducing an overview of subjects such as the drafting issues involved in drafting harmonised legislation following the Revised Treaty of Chaguaramas, non-municipal drafting instructions, concurrent jurisdictions, and inter-government agreements, treaties and conventions. I have been greatly indebted to Justice Duke Pollard of the Caribbean Court of Justice for helping with this initiative.

However I believe that care has to be taken that the Course remains one predominantly for teaching drafting within the Commonwealth syllabus and that the emphasis on treaties does not swing too far. I consider that the emphasis on treaties should be on *drafting treaties* and ancillary CARICOM matters. Other aspects of treaties could be dealt with separately for the region at a weekend or week's seminar. Otherwise too much time will be taken away from the main focus of the Course, that is, drafting.

Exams

In accordance with the experience of Professor Reed Dickerson narrated in Appendix F of his book *Fundamentals of Legal Drafting*, a final exam is held.[10] I believe this has great value in giving the Course a real focus. While most students approached the Course with a strong desire to learn and absorb all they could from it, the exam served to dispel any misplaced ideas of some that they were on a three-month rest cure. It must be emphasised, however, that most students took a keen and competitive interest in their personal grades. The University of Guyana supported the holding of an exam for the same reasons.

Part I of the exam took the form of a three-hour paper to test drafting skills with one question only, which involved the students drafting a short single subject Bill of about 10 clauses. Students could take in a dictionary/thesaurus, but no other books or aids.

Part II dealt with theory and principles in a $1^1/_2$-hour paper with a choice of questions, one section on straight factual matters and the other section allowing them to discuss drafting topics.

A week earlier the students had been given a class exam in identical format to allow them to become familiar with the format.

The object of the drafting exam (Part I) was to test whether the students had assimilated the rudiments of drafting without the help of precedents and the internet (which had been available to them for assignments); and whether they could prepare a very simple Bill in proper form.

[10]See n 4.

The expected results were for the top level of the students to produce by themselves workable drafts of legislation which would only require slight adjustments by an experienced drafter. The middle group were to be able to produce a result which was satisfactory in a learning context, but not exactly oven-ready.

The answers for Part I were marked taking into account whether the students had covered a range of essential items in the draft Bill; and also on general drafting style, syntax and clarity.

The simple Bills which the students were asked to draft included Bills to prohibit smoking in certain public places, to impose a tax on plastic bags supplied by retailers, and to regulate queuing in bakers' shops.

The exam on theory and principles (Part II) was to test whether students had learnt some of the basic principles of drafting which were taught throughout the Course.

Although most of the questions sought straight factual answers, some were expressed to allow discursive answers, but the answers were marked straightforwardly on the quantity and quality of the factual information given.

Some might describe Part II as academic, and up to a point that is right, as that is what it is meant to be – a test of whether the students have been attentive in class and have picked up some of the theory taught during the course. But the subjects in Part II (eg Thring's rules, savings provisions, using the active voice, vague words and Interpretation Acts) were all chosen for their bearing on practical drafting. If all the students knew and applied the answers to these questions (especially Thring's rules) they would be wonderful drafters. To bear that out, the best answers to Part II generally came from those who drafted good Bills in Part I. In summary, the whole of Part II, though testing theory and principles, was set with practical drafting considerations in mind.

The students

In general the students greatly impressed me with their skill, aptitude, application and enthusiasm and it was really good to see them making such progress with drafting. Some of them appeared natural drafters and I very much hope we can encourage them further.

Many drafters think that drafters are born, not made, and my experience teaching the subject bears that out. That is not to say that drafting courses are not necessary, because even the person born with the ability to draft needs tuition to develop and polish his or her skills. But while a course can provide a person who is not a born drafter with much information about the skills of drafting, grammar, syntax and parliamentary procedure and its politics, all of which may be useful in his or her career, and so of value to his or her country, I believe it is unlikely to change that person into an expert drafter. It is just possible that an old-fashioned apprenticeship might do so in 5–7 years, but not a 12-week course.

A necessary ingredient to be a successful drafter is high intelligence. But high intelligence does not guarantee successful drafting – there are many very able court lawyers and advocates who regrettably do not shine at drafting.

My aim in the Course was to train lawyers to produce a satisfactory draft of a piece of legislation of moderate length, which would only need a minimum of tweaking on checking by an experienced drafter. I believe almost half achieved that level, with most of the remainder not too far behind.

Follow-up

I am sorry to say that I am not at all sure from my contacts that most students are being afforded the necessary follow-up to gain maximum benefit from the Course for themselves and their country, though some certainly are.

As the Commonwealth Secretariat sponsored the Course, I believe it would be justified in following up what the students do after they have completed it, to ensure that they are placed in drafting positions.

I believe it is essential for individual countries to repay the amount of input and investment made by the Commonwealth Secretariat and actively use these newly trained drafters full-time in drafting offices, so that they can become fully qualified drafters.

For those in small countries, where there is no senior drafter to mentor them, or the senior is too busy, so that supervision is a problem (and I need no introduction to the problems of small states, having drafted in Seychelles and Tuvalu, and having been a Judge in Tonga), then there are ways of helping countries by mentoring etc, especially with the internet. The actual work of successful students could be supervised or inspected on a regular basis for a period of months or years by a Commonwealth Secretariat approved drafter.[11]

Alternatives

A 12-week residential course is enormously expensive in time and money. It also takes the students away from their offices for three whole months, which can be crucial in a small country, and also away from their families. The cost of putting up students for 12 weeks is substantial.

With these factors in mind, I have thought about the alternatives, although these too have disadvantages. One could be to deliver the training by distance learning on-line, but a great deal of work and time would be required to put the Course material into a suitable format for this. Nor would the students necessarily be able to devote the same amount of time to the course, and the teaching would lack the personal touch.

Another alternative would be to split up the Course. There could be:

> Two to three weeks' initial reading on preliminary and procedural parts of the Course. This could be done on-line in the home country and there might even be a preliminary exam on the material before joining the Course.
>
> Six weeks on core drafting subjects, principally actual drafting with many exercises. This would have to be done at the University.
>
> Three weeks on more advanced drafting, such as financial and tax legislation, statutory corporations, penal provisions, licensing and registration and treaties. This could be done at the University or on-line in the home country.

---

[11]The Commonwealth Secretariat has now started arranging mentoring for former students.

There would be a break in between the second and third parts. In this way it might help to split up the long period when students are away from their offices, but it might be harder for them to work from home and they could lose their focus on the Course.

Conclusion

There is now no doubt in my mind that, in educational terms, bearing in mind restrictions of time and finance, a course of around 12 weeks is the best option. It gives proper time for the exercises to be attempted in a meaningful way; and takes the students out of their normal environment so that they can devote themselves entirely to the Course.

But there remain many aspects of teaching drafting which can be improved on, especially harnessing modern technology, and I hope this article will stimulate some thinking about that.

Notes on contributor

Justice Robin Webster MBE has been drafting legislation since the late 1970s, when he joined the Office of the Solicitor to the Secretary of State for Scotland in Edinburgh. Secondments then followed as the Legal Draftsman to the Seychelles Government; Assistant Parliamentary Draftsman in the Lord Advocate's Department in London; Senior Parliamentary Counsel to the Kenya Government; and Attorney-General of the tiny Pacific island state of Tuvalu. He became a Judge of the Supreme Court of Tonga in 1988, being awarded the MBE for services to the judiciary in Tonga. In 1991 he returned home to Scotland and was an Employment Tribunal Chairman for several years. In 2004 he was asked to return to Tonga as Chief Justice, a post he held until 2006. Since then he has been Course Director of the Commonwealth Secretariat Caribbean Short Course in Legislative Drafting in 2007 and 2008.

The role of Parliamentary Counsel in legislative drafting

N.K. Nampoothiry

Joint Secretary and Legislative Counsel, Ministry of Law and Justice, Government of India

This article examines the role of the draftsperson in the legislative process. The services of a parliamentary counsel are utilized from the stage of making policy and drafting it in the form of legislative provisions. The main role of a parliamentary counsel is to give proper shape to the policies of the Government into legal provisions with adequate teeth for implementation. The legislative counsel should have sound knowledge of law and legal principles. The qualities of legislative drafters as well as the various stages of the drafting process are described, with particular reference to the position in India and Guyana. Ultimately, the task of a draftsperson is to help the country to have precise, readable and easily understandable laws useful to, and usable by, the public, to know and enforce their rights and privileges, perform their duties and be aware of their liabilities.

The Legislature is an essential organ of a democratic government. The main function of the Legislature is to make laws for the peace, progress and good government necessary for an orderly society in its jurisdiction. Legislation as a source of law has assumed greater importance in a society respecting the rule of law. Legislation is the main means by which all democratic countries give effect to their economic, social and political policies. Laws are generally made for the good of society and nowadays cover a wide variety of subjects, such as the ozone layer, the sea and the environment. The conduct of society and its well-being are thus regulated by law. In transforming the policies into binding rules of conduct, the Legislature has to clearly, concisely and in a systematic manner lay down legislation, and the parliamentary counsel plays a significant role in this process.

It is the job of the parliamentary counsel to draft the laws for the concerned Legislature. In India, a parliamentary counsel is designated as a legislative counsel. 'Legal draftsman' or 'legislative draftsperson' and 'legal drafter' are other nomenclatures given to the person doing the job of a parliamentary counsel. The laws are, therefore, drafted very carefully and methodically by experienced and capable draftspersons. In order to maintain the consistency of language and uniformity of form the draftsperson adopts a method of presentation which enables the lawyers, judges, legislators and the common man to understand the laws without doubt and without any ambiguity. If individual lawyers attempt to draft a law it may not necessarily have all these qualities and consistency with the existing statute book. Hence in all modern democratic countries, especially in Commonwealth countries, the role of professionally experienced legal draftspersons has assumed significance.

Even though legislation is the domain of the Legislatures, yet the executive limb of the Government plays a major role in making binding laws. Based on the various inputs received by it, the policy framework for parliamentary legislation is formulated by the Government. Necessary subsidiary legislation containing the details required to give effect to the provisions of the statute are also made by the executive, and the parliamentary counsel has a significant role to play in drafting such legislation as well.

The services of a parliamentary counsel are utilized from the stage of making policy and drafting it in the form of legislative provisions. The main role of a parliamentary counsel is to give proper shape to the policies of the Government into legal provisions with adequate teeth for implementation. The policies are to be interwoven into the existing statute book in a logical sequence and as accurately and clearly as possible and in a language which is unambiguous and understandable by all. It must also be borne in mind that in a normative hierarchy the legislation is subordinate to the Constitution of a country, and the secondary legislation is subordinate to the relevant statutes.

The establishment of an office of parliamentary counsel with an adequate number of drafters as part of the Government machinery has many advantages, compared to getting the Bills and subsidiary legislation drafted by lawyers from outside the drafting department. Some of the advantages are listed below:

(i) there will be uniformity in form and presentation with which all consumers –lawyers, legislators, administrators, judiciary, litigants and the affected persons – are familiar;
(ii) the drafters will be specialised and will be available at all times;
(iii) time-bound and urgent legislation, like Ordinances and proclamations, could be drafted as per the priority of the Government of the day;
(iv) as the drafters work in a team, the absence of one drafter will not disturb the legislative programme of the Government;
(v) there will be continuity and adequate accountability in the work;
(vi) there will be no need to search for suitable drafters each time, thus saving considerable time;
(vii) the drafters will have all required tools and precedents readily available to undertake any fresh proposal within a given time frame;
(viii) the drafters, being public servants, would be governed by the conduct rules and thus Government could work out confidential proposals like enhancement of certain taxes, duties, etc.
(ix) Subsidiary legislation would be conceptualized, formulated and drafted quickly and professionally;
(x) the services of the drafters will be available to assist the various parliamentary Committees and this will help the Committees to redraw the Bills quickly and present them to the Legislature. It will also enable the smooth passage of the Bills in the Legislature, making themselves available in the official gallery to assist the Ministers piloting the Bills.

Qualities and experience of a legislative draftsperson

The increasing legislative activity of the Governments has undoubtedly increased the need for a sufficient number of proficient and experienced draftspersons available to the Government for carrying out their policies in a time-bound manner.

Legislative drafting is a means of communication. Hence, the legislative counsel should have sound knowledge of law and legal principles. As the job of the legislative draftsperson is to translate policies into legislative provisions, to be introduced in the appropriate Legislature in the form of Bills, the person should have sound knowledge of:

- (i) the Constitution and domestic law of the country, and the international law, including international commitments and comparative law of the region;
- (ii) the rules of procedure and practice followed by the Legislature;
- (iii) the rules of interpretation and procedural law adopted by the Courts as well as judicial decisions;
- (iv) the language in which the draftsperson is drafting; and
- (v) the custom and usage having the force of law in the jurisdiction.

The draftsperson should first and foremost be an able lawyer who has adequate experience in the legal profession. The person should also have adequate interest and aptitude in legislative drafting, and should be systematic and meticulous. The draftsperson should have a cool and inquisitive mind and the capacity to work under pressure. As the job description will require the draftsperson to deal with a variety of subjects, it may not be possible to become expert in all of them. Hence the draftsperson may have to gain an understanding of concepts and technical aspects from the subject experts.

While the draftsperson should not take on the role of a policy maker, there is a duty to help the policy maker to shape the policy, and to identify the gaps where adequate instructions are lacking. The draftsperson may hold conferences with the subject experts and other persons who will be giving policy inputs, in order to better comprehend the purpose of the legislation, what it proposes to remedy and to give shape to the policy adequately and comprehensively.

The draftsperson should have an inquiring, critical, imaginative and open mind to understand different viewpoints from the perspective of various consumers of the laws. The person has a duty to foresee possible eventualities connected with the issue involved in drafting and if necessary advise the sponsoring ministry to improve the substantive policy. The proposals should be examined and the draftsperson must be satisfied that they are capable of being implemented, fit into the scheme of the existing statute book and suggest solutions to any danger areas.

The draftsperson should have the ability to work with colleagues and persons of other disciplines and the ability to accept constructive criticism and advice from others.

A person intending to become a legislative counsel should be ready to dedicate time and energy to the profession and develop a special aptitude for it. Efficiency in drafting comes not by mere mastery of the rules, but by the exercise of a faculty of the mind which can be described as skill or a natural gift. The sense of use of language is the main qualification of a competent draftsperson. A good lawyer need not be a good draftsperson. Knowledge of law could be acquired by studies, intelligence, ability to grasp and memorize, and judgement. But the ability to draft is developed like that of an artist. The draftspersons is a creative artist dealing with policies and conceptualizing and translating them into legislative provisions in an eloquent and logical sequence.

A good draftsperson is a wordsmith and a miser. The person has to see that every word used gives out a clear and unambiguous meaning and is fit to the given situation. A word once let loose cannot be recalled. Every word used has to pass the test of the Legislature, the stakeholders and the Judiciary.

Legislative drafting

Legislation is normally introduced in the Legislature by way of a Bill. It needs no emphasis that the primary object of the legislative draftsperson is to express the provisions of a proposed legislation very clearly and unequivocally, as it reflects the intention of the Legislature. It is, therefore, very important that statutes should be drafted very carefully and meticulously. The ambiguities which arise from imperfections in drafting Bills are comparatively few. They may be classified as those which are accidental, being mistakes of the draftsperson and those which may be considered more or less intentional. The accidental imperfections could be ascribed to the complexity and novelty of many of the subjects which have to be dealt with by the draftsperson at any given time due to pressure from the clients.

Although a methodical drafting process involves several stages of drafting, yet in view of the priority which may be given and time allotted by the Government, the drafter may have to skip or combine the stages. In India, a proposal received in the Legislative Department is supposed to be cleared within 15 days to six weeks depending upon the complexity of the matter, and when several proposals of a priority nature are there at a time and have to be cleared at various levels, the task becomes more onerous and the quality is bound to suffer. Generally, almost all draftsperson consider the following stages mentioned by GC Thornton in his *Legislative Drafting* as the main stages of drafting:[1]

(1) Understanding.
(2) Analysis.
(3) Design.
(4) Composition.
(5) Scrutiny.

In India, a Ministry may have one or more Departments. As per the allocation of business given to various Ministries/departments, a decision as to whether any legislative measure is to be processed depends upon the Ministry concerned. In case a Ministry/Department considers that a legislative measure is to be brought before Parliament, it consults the stakeholders and initiates the proposal in the shape of a Note for Cabinet. The draft Note for Cabinet is circulated to all other Ministries/departments which may also be concerned with the subject matter in one

[1](4th edn LexisNexis, London 1996).

way or other seeking their views/comments/concurrence. In all proposals involving legislation, the Ministry of Law and Justice is invariably consulted. The Law Ministry examines the proposal from legal and Constitutional points of view, and the legislative counsel offers a draft Bill to be appended to the Note for Cabinet. In formulating the draft Bill, the legislative counsel holds discussions with the officers of the administrative Ministry and subject experts. The drafting is done by a group of drafters of various ranks. After receipt of the comments/concurrence of other Ministries/Departments, the Note for Cabinet is suitably revised and the same is placed before Cabinet for approval. The administrative Ministry also informs Cabinet of its counter-comments on the suggestions/comments received by it. Cabinet at times scrutinizes the proposal by a Group of Ministers before approval is accorded.

Once the draft Bill is approved by Cabinet in principle, the legislative counsel scrutinizes the Bill once more and carries out modifications of a purely drafting or consequential nature. The legislative counsel also settles the other documents required to be appended to the text of the Bill as per convention and the rules of procedure of Parliament. The legislative counsel should be well conversant with the rules of procedure and practice in both Houses of Parliament, and the Constitutional provisions governing legislation, including the legislative competence of Parliament. The knowledge and experience of the draftsperson in this area would be immensely helpful in settling the documents expeditiously. Money Bills are to be invariably introduced in the House of the People. Unless waiver is granted by the presiding officer of the House, seven days' notice and circulation of the Bill amongst the Members of Parliament two clear days in advance are required for introduction of a Bill in Parliament. The introduction could be opposed on grounds of legislative competence and/or non-compliance with the rules of procedure. Hence the draftsperson should be careful about these aspects, as it involves the prestige of the Government if the introduction of the Bill is forestalled on these technical grounds.

If the Bill is not an amending piece of legislation and the number of clauses exceeds 25, an arrangement of clauses is appended at the beginning of the Bill to serve as an index to the Bill. As per the subject matter and length of the Bill, the draftsperson divides the Bill into Chapters or Parts for convenience. Every Bill will have a Statement of Objects and Reasons appended to it immediately after the Bill portion. This is a document signed by the Minister who may be piloting the Bill in Parliament and it contains a brief statement explaining the objectives of the proposed legislation and the reasons for the proposed legislative measure. If the provisions of the Bill are of a difficult or complicated nature, a note called 'notes on clauses' explaining the various provisions of the Bill is appended to the Statement of Objects and Reasons. This is written in simple layman's language. If the provisions of the Bill have any financial implication, a financial memorandum drawing attention to the particular clauses involving such expenditure is appended to the Bill. The Memorandum explains the likely recurring and non-recurring expenditure from the Consolidated Fund of India separately. The clauses involving expenditure are to be printed in bold style.

If the Bill contains any provision empowering the Central Government, State Government or any authority to make subsidiary legislation to give effect to the provisions of the proposed legislation, a Memorandum Regarding Delegated

Legislation is appended. This Memorandum invites attention to the specific clauses of the Bill involving delegated or subsidiary legislation. It also contains a declaration as to the nature of the delegation, why provisions could not be made in the Bill itself, and a note as to the character of the delegation. If the Bill amends an existing statute, extracts of the existing provisions which may be affected by the proposal are appended to the Bill. If the Bill repeals and replaces an Ordinance promulgated by the President, a memorandum explaining the modifications made in the provisions of the Ordinance is also appended. In case the Bill contains provisions on taxation requiring immediate implementation, a declaration that it is to give immediate effect certain specified provisions of the Bill be printed immediately after the text of the Bill. This is in pursuance of the Provisional Collection of Taxes Act, 1931.

The pages are numbered and the text on each page is line numbered every five lines. The amendment which may be moved in the House also refers to the page number, clause number and the line numbers involved. The marginal notes are to be printed outside the text. The marginal notes on odd pages are printed on the right margin and those on even pages are printed on the left margin. Every Bill is in the English language and it is invariably accompanied by the Hindi version, which is the official language of the Union.

The formalities for Private Member's Bills are the same as those for Government Bills. The official draftspersons do not assist in drafting Private Member's Bills. For reasons of brevity, the other requirements are not explained here.

The practice followed in respect of Bills introduced in the National Assembly of the Co-operative Republic of Guyana is simpler. Every Government Bill introduced in the National Assembly of Guyana will contain an arrangement of sections at the beginning and an Explanatory Memorandum duly signed by the Minister who will be piloting the Bill in the National Assembly at the end. No other document is required to be attached to the Bill.

The format of a Bill will depend upon the rules of procedure or Standing Orders of the Legislature which, in the Commonwealth countries, are similar. But based on the subject matter of the Bill the contents may vary. In amending Bills, the sequence of clauses will be in the order of the provisions of the principal Act being amended. Based on the Indian National Green Tribunal Bill, 2009 introduced in the House of the People on 31 July 2009, a model of the format of a Bill is given below:

Arrangement of clauses

Chapter I
Preliminary Clauses

1. Short title and commencement.
2. Definitions.

Chapter II
Establishment of the Tribunal

3. Establishment of Tribunal.
4. Composition of Tribunal.
5. Qualifications for appointment of Chairperson, Judicial Member and Expert Member.
6. Appointment of Chairperson, Judicial Member and Expert Member.
7. Term of office and other conditions of service of Chairperson, Judicial Member and Expert Member.
8. Resignation.

9. Salaries, allowances and other terms and conditions of service.
10. Removal and suspension of Chairperson, Judicial Member and Expert Member.
11. To act as Chairperson of Tribunal or to discharge his functions in certain circumstances.
12. Staff of Tribunal.
13. Financial and administrative powers of Chairperson.

Chapter III
Jurisdiction, powers and proceedings of the Tribunal

14. Tribunal to settle disputes.
15. Relief, compensation and restitution.
16. Tribunal to have appellate jurisdiction.
17. Liability to pay relief or compensation in certain cases.
18. Application or appeal to Tribunal.
19. Procedure and powers of Tribunal
20. Decision to be taken by majority.
21. Finality of order.
22. Cost.
23. Deposit of amount payable for damage to environment.
24. Execution of award or order or Tribunal.

Chapter IV
Penalty

25. Penalty for failure to comply with orders of Tribunal.
26. Offences by companies.
27. Offences by Government department.

Chapter V
Miscellaneous

28. Bar of jurisdiction.
29. Cognizance of offences.
30. Members and staff of Tribunal to be public servants.
31. Protection of action taken in good faith.
32. Act to have overriding effect.
33. Power to amend Schedule I.
34. Power to make rules.
35. Amendment of certain enactments.
36. Power to remove difficulties.
37. Repeal and savings.

Schedule I.
Schedule II.
Schedule III.

While considering the arrangements of clauses, we are reminded of the following rules laid down by Lord Thring in his 'Practical Legislation':

Rule 1. Provisions declaring the law should be separated from and take precedents of provisions relating to the administration of the law.

Rule 2. The simpler proposition should precede the more complex and in an ascending scale of propositions the less should come before the greater.

Rule 3. Principal provisions should be separated from subordinate provisions. The latter should be placed towards the end of the Act, while the former should occupy their proper position in the narrative occurrence to which they refer.

Rule 4.(a) Local or exceptional provisions, (b) temporary provisions, and (c) provision relating to repeal of Acts should be separated from the other enactments, and placed by themselves under separate headings.

Stages discussed

The first thing that a draftsperson has to establish is what the client wants, and how it can be accommodated having regard to the Constitutionality and legislative competence of the Legislature. The draftsperson also has to decide whether an amendment in an existing statute is sufficient, or a fresh principal enactment is required. Sometimes the proposal needs no legislation, or it could be given effect by subsidiary legislation under an existing statute. Based on familiarity with customary law, the Constitution and statute book, the draftsperson will be able to guide the client quickly. Sometimes fundamental rights or certain legal hurdles may stand against the proposal. In complicated cases having far-reaching consequences, or cases involving the violation of fundamental or human rights, an extensive study is to be conducted in order to determine how to go about addressing those issues. One should avoid legislating against morality or public good. Once the draftsperson understands the proposition thoroughly and is satisfied about the desirability and mode of carrying out the legislative work, the draftsperson may proceed to the next stage of analysis.

At the stage of analysis, the draftsperson will consider the methodology to be adopted in giving effect to the proposal. If extensive changes are to be made in some existing statute, it would be better to repeal and re-enact the same with necessary modifications.

The next stage is the design of the legislation. Once the draftsperson has understood the proposal and its implication, the legislation may be designed. If it is sufficiently long or complicated in nature, it is better to prepare a legislative scheme containing an outline or broad contents and shape of the legislation. Based on experience and intimacy with the statute book, the draftsperson will be able to design the legislation based on some existing statute with necessary modifications. The statute book should be considered as a single coherent whole and not a collection of untidy pieces.

Once the design is worked out, the draftsperson should undertake the composition of the Bill, which should be scrutinized and revised as necessary. Ideally, the draft is also shown to two or more other draftspersons and comments invited. The draftsperson should check up the arrangements of clauses and ensure that the provisions are arranged as per the subject matter of each chapter and there is sequence and continuity in the presentation. Clauses must be numbered consecutively by numerals throughout the Bill, whether the Bill is divided into various Chapters or Parts or not. One idea should be put in one section and in one grammatical sentence. If an idea cannot be put in one sentence, the section may be divided into subsections where one subsection may contain one sentence. Subsections may be numbered with numerals in brackets. Long sections and subsections should be avoided. The cases and conditions should be set out first, followed by the rule, unless the rule is to apply to several cases or conditions .When cases and conditions are expressed, cases should precede the conditions.

In India, Guyana and certain other jurisdictions, the interpretation clause or the definition clause is put in the preliminary chapter or at the beginning after the short title clause. An expression having a special meaning occurring at least once in the Bill could be defined in the Bill. Normally a definition is for the purpose of avoiding repetition or ambiguity. Punctuation should be kept to a minimum and as per the practice followed by the draftspersons of the country. Different words or expressions should not be used to denote the same thing. A change in language means a change in intention. The statute should be able to be construed without punctuation. Use of provisos should be avoided, as far as practicable. The marginal headings or marginal notes should be short, distinctive and capable of being catchwords. They should be in substantial form. When delegation is contemplated, adequate guidelines to the delegate should be contained in the provision as unbridled delegation will not stand the test of judicial scrutiny. Matters of procedure or of details could be left to the executive to make subsidiary legislation as they are flexible, and could be changed as frequently as the situation may warrant. But adequate guidelines and substantive policy should be laid down in the enactment itself. The draftsperson should keep in mind the rules laid down in the Interpretation and General Clauses legislation, the decisions of the Courts and the general rules of interpretation of statutes applied by the Courts in the country.

Thus the task of a draftsperson is to help the country to have precise, readable and easily understandable laws useful to, and usable by, the public, to know and enforce their rights and privileges, perform their duties and be aware of their liabilities.

Notes on contributor

N.K. Nampoothiry is Joint Secretary and Legislative Counsel at the Ministry of Law and Justice, Government of India, New Delhi and formerly Legal Expert and Advanced Legislative draftsperson, Attorney General's Chambers, Ministry of Legal Affairs, Government of the Co-operative Republic of Guyana, Georgetown.

Prioritising legislative proposals in the legislative process

Richard C. Nzerem

Hon. Director, Sir William Dale Centre for Legislative Studies, Institute of Advanced Legal Studies of the University of London

The most important duty of a government is to create a conducive environment in which citizens can meaningfully participate in the development of the country and also develop their personal capabilities to the fullest extent possible. This article examines the sometimes problematic issue, not generally seen as critically important, of prioritising legislative proposals and, in passing, briefly touches on the catalytic role of the legislative drafter as an agent for change and social transformation. Anyone who has knowledge of legislative drafting will confirm that the drafter is by no means a completely free agent in respect of the manner in which to carry out the task of drafting. Of necessity, there is a political angle to what the drafter does and the reason for this is that the legislative programme of a government lies at the heart of the government's domestic activities. Bills are political instruments as well as legal instruments. Seen in this light, the drafter is an important player in the machinery of government, as otherwise it would not be possible to translate government policies into effective law.

General introduction

In most modern societies, the laws that govern human behaviour usually exist in a variety of forms. The forms include legislation and 'unwritten' rules such as custom and convention. Today, however, the most important laws that govern human behaviour consist largely of written laws that we call legislation. Such laws are usually made by a body that has the power to make laws and this is a practice that is common in jurisdictions that share the common law tradition.

However, the arrangements for making written laws and the nature of the body that has the power to make such laws vary from country to country. These would usually depend on the constitution of the country in question. In a democratic society, that power will usually be vested in an elected government.[1] In very simple and practical terms, the most important duty of a government is to create a conducive environment in which citizens can meaningfully participate in the development of the country and also develop their personal capabilities to the fullest extent possible.

---

[1]Government is used here in a generic sense to mean the sovereign power of the state to legislate without making the constitutional distinctions between the legislative, executive and judicial functions.

This article examines the sometimes problematic issue, not generally seen as critically important, of prioritising legislative proposals and, in passing, briefly touches on the catalytic role of the legislative drafter as an agent for change and social transformation.

The power to govern and, in the process of doing so, to introduce new laws shapes the government's exercise of executive power. In many countries that practice parliamentary democracy the exercise of executive power has often also involved the exercise of legislative power. If it chooses to do so, a government can use its power to govern through laws that achieve good governance and thereby bring about social change and transformation or it can use that power arbitrarily. In the latter case the result could be that the society and its institutions are exposed to becoming dysfunctional.

As the person employed to prepare draft written rules before they can be passed into laws, it is easy to see that the drafter is an important player in the machinery of government as otherwise it would not be possible to translate government policies into effective law. The authority of the drafter to carry out this important exercise derives from a request that the drafter receives, usually from a government department. This request comes in the form of 'drafting instructions' to draft a specific legislation.

The need to prioritise

The phenomenon of the use of legislation as a deliberate instrument of choice to determine the shape of society is not a subject that has received as much attention as it deserves. Many notable authors in the field of legislative drafting agree that the function of a drafter is not simply to translate government policy into written laws. It is evident from some of these writings that in the law-making process, contrary to popular belief, the drafter plays an important role with respect to both the form and content of a law. Many agree that the drafter's task is not merely to communicate the instructions he or she has received to the general public through the medium of legislation.

In the Preface to the first edition of his acclaimed work on legislative drafting, Thornton was emphatic on the need for the drafter to develop an obsession to draft so as to be readily understood. The drafter's task, Thornton said, is not only to 'determine' the law but also to 'communicate' it.[2] The form and content of legislation, in his view, must be linked otherwise the dual task of translating and communicating instructions the drafter has received cannot be effectively carried out. Implicit in this view, however, is that it should never be thought that it is ever the function of a drafter either to initiate legislative policy or to determine legislative policy as properly understood. That rests squarely in the domain of the instructing authority, namely the government.

Legislative policy is very often rooted in the rough and tumble of politics and can be traced to the manifesto promises made by political parties at election time. It is natural that a political party that has been elected to office on the back

---

[2]See GC Thornton, *Legislative Drafting* (Butterworths, London 1979) viii. Thornton's choice of emphasis in this regard contrasts sharply with other writers in so far as drafters are not usually given the power to 'determine' laws.

of promises it has made during an election campaign, if it wants to be re-elected at the next election, will wish to demonstrate that it has made an effort to fulfil at least some of its pre-election promises. The power of legislation as an instrument for bringing about social change cannot be doubted or underestimated. Against the knowledge that the public usually treats more seriously government policy that is in the form of a law especially if that law has practical legal consequences, the ruling party, through the appropriate government department, will issue drafting instructions for the necessary draft legislation to be prepared in respect of a policy that it wishes to implement. If a political party has made many election promises and decides to legislate to implement all of those policies, it will probably end up having a very crowded and unsustainable legislative programme.

As a consequence of the pressures of the job, the life of a drafter is not an easy one. The profession of legislative drafting is one discipline of law that requires complete devotion, focused attention and consistent hard work. In drafting any new legislation the drafter has to undertake an in-depth study of the issues involved, has to interact with policy makers, relevant experts, politicians and stakeholders in order to keep abreast of developments past, present and future.[3] In addition, the drafter has to deal with many pressures. Invariably, the reasons for the laws that he or she is called upon to draft do not arise in a vacuum. A drafter has to bear in mind the reasons for the legislation. He or she has to consider the state of society as it was in the past, as it is in the present and as it is desired that it should be in the future. This means that the drafter has to draft not only to deal with the problems of the past and present but must also think of the future by laying down rules of conduct for the guidance of society.[4] What this amounts to is that the dividing line between policy and the substance or content of law enacted to implement that policy may be blurred and that the drafter often cannot escape being involved in policy considerations.

The context of legislation: law, development and good governance

It is important for the drafter to be always mindful not only of the reasons for a law but also of the context in which that law has to operate. This means, for instance, that there will be such issues as law and development, law and good governance as well as other matters, including form, to consider.

The law ought to be used as an agent to facilitate development, social change and social transformation, especially in the face of such powerfully overwhelming new forms of potential disempowerment as globalisation. The need for the law to be proactive in facilitating development, social change and social transformation is more evident in countries going through a period of transition. Typical examples of

---

[3]See BR Atre, Preface to *Legislative Drafting* (2nd edn Universal Law Publishing Co, Delhi 2006) v, and as to the many problems a drafter faces see VCRAC Crabbe, *Legislative Drafting* (Cavendish, London 1993) 1.

[4]The position is not made any easier by the need for the drafter to avoid unwittingly giving credence to a popular perception that the drafter is 'undoubtedly the cause of half the litigation' engendered by laws composed by the drafter and to also avoid becoming an even easier target for critics who have little appreciation of the job of a drafter.

this are where, as a result of some kind of turmoil such as endemic civil disorder, war, a major natural disaster or even emergence from colonial rule, society has become dysfunctional and the normal institutions of society can no longer be relied upon to function effectively.

Human rights and social justice

Some jurisdictions now require that laws must be so drafted as to be compliant in certain respects, such as human rights, in line with treaty obligations that have overriding effect on national legislation.[5] The suggestion is not that the drafter must attempt to cover every possibility. That would be impossible as it is not possible to foretell the future.

Many modern constitutions set out deliberately to ensure that the constitution itself is used as a tool for securing social justice. For instance, many newly independent states that wish to demonstrate their democratic credentials give themselves constitutions that contain provisions that are often described generally as the directive principles of state policy, as distinct from, for instance, those contained in a separate Bill of Rights which may also form part of the constitution.[6] An illustration of the relevance of context and the need for the drafter to keep this in view is the way the 1996 South African Constitution has been used to achieve the transformation of apartheid South Africa into a democratic South Africa.

By and large, the law drafters of the apartheid era generally were not able to rise above the challenges presented by the drafting instructions that they were given. Most were virtual prisoners of, and succumbed to, the prevailing constitutional arrangements. They drafted laws that were intended to maintain the status quo. This is in sharp contrast to their post-apartheid counterparts at least some of whom, both white and black, had fought apartheid in the courts against daunting odds. Many of these have been able to take advantage of the political and socially

[5]The UK Human Rights Act 1998. Section 19 of the Act requires a Minister responsible for a Bill before Parliament to make a statement, inter alia, that in his or her view the provisions of the Bill are compatible with the European Human Rights Convention.

[6]See for instance, the constitutions of India, Part IV Articles 36-51: Directive Principles of State Policy; Nigeria, Chapter II Articles 14–25: Fundamental Objectives and Directive Principles of State Policy; Papua New Guinea, National Goals and Directive Principles; Sri Lanka, Chapter VI: Directive Principles of State Policy and Fundamental Duties: Articles 27–29; Uganda, National Objectives and Directive Principles of State Policy: General, Parts I–XXIX; and by contrast Chapter II of the Interim National Constitution of the Republic of Sudan Guiding Principles and Directives, Articles 10–22. Article 22 is a Savings Article rendering the principles and directives enumerated unenforceable per se whereas the Bill of Rights enacted in the same Constitution in Articles 27–48 expressly provides that these Articles are a 'Covenant' between the Government and the people of Sudan and are enforceable. See also 'Advancing Human Rights in South Africa', 1992 by the eminent South African jurist Albie Sachs at 31 – where he decries the fact that social and economic rights are excluded and made redundant by people who do not wish their taken-for-granted lifestyle to be disturbed or diluted.

pluralistic liberated society that rose from the ashes of apartheid to try to right old wrongs.[7]

After the sun had set on the 1994 provisional Constitution of South Africa, it was not surprising that the legitimate expectations of the opponents of apartheid influenced the calculations of the drafters of the 1996 Constitution. These calculations have continued to loom large in both the form and content of post-apartheid legislation. It was against the background of a widely acknowledged need for change which reflected the aspirations of the new diverse society that the 1996 Constitution was drafted.

No longer shackled by the apartheid constitution and in recognition of the need for change, drafters in the new South Africa have sought to exercise their proper functions without fear while at the same time remaining faithful to the individual specific instructions they receive.[8] In this context, it has been possible for the drafter, while remaining faithful to the 'instructions', to draft in a way that promotes social justice. However, it would be misleading to suggest that every situation is amenable to the drafter's intervention on policy issues, just as it would be wrong to expect that legislative precedents would work in every situation.[9]

The essence of prioritisation

Prioritisation is a two-stage exercise. It is carried out at two different levels, in the order in which they occur, first by the executive authority when it has decided that it is necessary to legislate and then by the drafting establishment which it instructs to draft the necessary legislation. In the normal course of carrying out its duty to govern, the government, with the finite resources at its disposal has to address a myriad of social problems and has to respond to the multiple demands made on it. It must provide adequate health facilities, schools, an efficient transportation system, housing and other social and political needs.

In seeking to provide these needs, the government, therefore, must make a conscious decision on where and how it allocates resources. It must decide the order in which to introduce the legislative measures necessary for implementing its policies. In other words, it must prioritise the subject matter of the legislative

[7]Prominent among these was Arthur Chaskalson, SC, founder of the South African Legal Resources Centre, who was one of the principal drafters of the new South African Constitution and who subsequently became President of South Africa's Constitutional Court. It is apparent that Chaskalson shared the views of many other eminent South Africans who fought against apartheid, that the system of justice in South Africa had been so discredited by its role in upholding apartheid that it might not withstand the transition to democracy. This would have weighed heavily in the minds of the drafters when they were drafting the new constitution.

[8]For an incisive examination and appreciation of the role of the drafter in constitution drafting see Jeremy Sarkin, 'The Drafting of South Africa's Final Constitution from a Human-Rights Perspective' (1999) 47 American Journal of Comparative Law 67. One of the innovative characteristics of the South African Constitution is the inclusion of the concept of the right to administrative justice which is justiciable.

[9]For an examination of a less successful attempt, in circumstances similar to the South African experience, to use legislation as an instrument of change see Theunis Roux, 'Constitutional Property Rights Review in Southern Africa: Record of the Zimbabwe Supreme Court' (1996) 8 African Journal of International and Comparative Law 755.

proposal in question in terms of its importance to the government. If it decides to legislate to implement a particular policy or programme, it may find, for a variety of reasons, that its best intentions are insufficient to guarantee easy passage of the legislation. One prerequisite in determining legislative priorities is that the government must, among other things, bear in mind the parliamentary time available which it ignores at its peril.

The process of prioritisation

After the government has decided to legislate in order to implement its programme, the drafting establishment which is always under pressure to produce the necessary draft legislation also has to decide in what order to produce the drafts. In many jurisdictions, the resources placed at the disposal of the drafting establishment are often inadequate. The drafter, in turn, may therefore also be under pressure to prioritise in order not to waste scarce resources and time on relatively insignificant bills.

Viewed in this light, prioritisation is largely a political rather than a technical matter. It shapes the government's exercise of state power, in particular its legislative power. If it is accepted that the drafter's role involves making appropriate inputs, it would follow almost by definition that the drafter would be involved in helping those primarily responsible for policy to determine priorities in pursuing legislation as a means of addressing problems and bringing about social change.

Generally speaking, in every government some central government agency exercises the function of vetting all legislative proposals to ensure that they are in accordance with government policy. Often this central agency is located in Cabinet Office and will usually comprise a committee of senior cabinet ministers who decide which proposals should receive legislative priority.

In some jurisdictions, however, there is no such central agency. In such cases, prioritisation is done by the drafting establishment which receives from a variety of government departments drafting instructions that are sometimes conflicting and incoherent.[10] And yet it is surprising that there is little writing in the field of legislative drafting that gives the subject of prioritisation the serious attention that it deserves. The only attention given to it is often merely incidental to the legislative process.[11]

Clearly, there is advantage in ensuring that legislation is both coherent and relevant to the needs of society. This can best be achieved only if available resources

[10]See AW Seidman, RB Seidman and Nalin Abeyesekere, *Legislative Drafting for Democratic Social Change* (Kluwer International, Boston 2001) 53–54 where they express the view that the absence of clear cut criteria or procedures is more likely to lead to haphazard prioritisation. This, however, need not be so, especially if the drafting establishment is well organised and is staffed by experienced drafters who are fully conversant with the government's general policy and legislative programme. Where the government's legislative policy is clearly defined and already prioritised in its legislative programme, the drafter would have no discretion in the matter or, at best, his/her discretion would be extremely limited. Where the priorities have not been so predetermined, the drafter has discretion which would then respond to both objective and subjective pressures.

[11]Ibid 55 et seq.

are utilised to maximum advantage. Further, there is a good chance that legislation would be more relevant to the needs of society if certain conditions exist. First, it would be helpful if there are clearly identifiable means, such as through a central agency, for prioritising legislation and, second, it would also be very helpful if there are established criteria for doing so.

Whatever the case, it is important that prioritisation should be based upon public interest. It should not be based upon narrow departmental or sectional interests or upon a misconception of the proper role a drafter. It should also be flexible enough to take into account changing circumstances. If it is not flexible enough, it will not be able to address emerging social problems.[12]

The institutions for prioritising legislation

The agency and location of the agency responsible for determining prioritisation will vary from one jurisdiction to another. Of necessity, this will depend on the constitutional arrangements in the jurisdiction concerned. In some jurisdictions, it may be the Cabinet or a committee of the Cabinet, often the Cabinet Committee on Legislation. In others the agency may be located within a government department where senior officials will take into account the range of projects that require legislative backing and all relevant background information in the possession of the department that will justify inclusion of the legislative proposal in the priority list.[13]

Background information could include whether the project has already received Cabinet approval as part of the overall legislative programme. If such approval has not been given, there is a risk that departmental resources may be wasted on projects that cannot be guaranteed to meet Cabinet approval. It could also include an assessment of the chances of the draft bill surviving vis-à-vis other projects competing for legislative backing as well as the rigours of the often crowded parliamentary time table. This is further illustration of the proposition that prioritisation takes place at more than one level in the unravelling of the legislative programme and the process of legislation itself.

The essentially political nature of prioritisation requires that those who make the decision must have a good knowledge and appreciation of both the resource and technical constraints. They should also have regard to some criteria on which to proceed in making their decision.

Criteria for prioritisation[14]

Commonsense would suggest that a prioritising agency should carefully weigh proposed projects and draft legislation for implementing those projects against their relative economic and social costs and benefits. It would help the prioritising

---

[12]Ibid 56.
[13]See David Miers and Alan Page, *Legislation* (Sweet & Maxwell, London 1982) chapter 2, 25–36.
[14]For an in-depth examination of considerations that might influence the decision to legislate, see generally, Seidman et al (n 10) 57–79.

agency therefore to have on hand information concerning the resources available, both financial and human.

The power of legislation as an instrument for bringing about social change cannot be doubted or underestimated. In order to understand the proper role of a law and how the drafter relates to that role, it is important to also understand that the law does not operate in a vacuum. There will always be a reason for legislation. The reason for legislating may be to change existing law that is proving inadequate to deal with contemporary problems. It may be to repeal an existing law and to remove it from the statute book. The reason for repealing the law in question may be because the problem has now been resolved. It may also be to initiate a completely new law for regulating behaviour in respect of a novel area of activity, for example in order to regulate commercial space travel.

Prioritisation criteria may be examined under the following headings:

(a) The gravity of the social problem being addressed, such as improving the quality of life of the majority and alleviating poverty

Even in a functioning democracy where the institutions of society command the respect of citizens generally, there are still problems that need addressing almost on a daily basis. Law and order will command attention as will education and health. How law makers judge the performance of their national institutions may depend on the importance that they attach to the role these institutions should play in shaping the social conditions in their jurisdiction. Their ability to make this judgement meaningfully and authoritatively will require a certain level of economic literacy. The economic life and prosperity of every society is inextricably bound up with the ability of that society to harness its resources and productive energies to the fullest extent possible.

There are compelling reasons why it would make good sense to give a high priority to legislative proposals that seek to enhance the welfare of the general population. Similarly, there would be advantage in giving a high priority to legislative proposals that are intended to improve the efficiency of national institutions that underpin good governance. This would be particularly so in, for instance, poor developing countries and countries in transition from one-party state to multi-party parliamentary democracy. It could also be the same for a country changing from a command economy to a free market economy.

The experience of many such countries, especially those that had been colonised and only recently gained sovereign independence, has not been a particularly happy one. Some discover, immediately after gaining independence, that like any other sovereign state, they now have to find their own way in the world. In one fell swoop, they have to deal with providing a wide range of services that they did not have to concern themselves with – hospitals, schools, roads, water and electricity supplies, cultural and leisure programmes, retirement and old age pensions and all the other amenities and attributes of decent life in a modern state.

The experience of many of these 'transition' countries is that almost invariably they find themselves in a debt trap. Often, the problems are caused by a combination of poor political leadership and lack of probity in the management of national resources. Sometimes, the problems are exacerbated by manipulative outside 'help'.[15] Not least of such manipulative help will come from unsuspected quarters such as the established trading blocs or organisations and international financial institutions including the WTO, the IMF and the World Bank. Much has been written about the crippling effect help from some good Samaritan institutions has on the developmental aspirations of hapless developing economies.[16]

Very commonly, the practice of some financial institutions is to impose stringent pre-conditions. These usually come in the form of prescribing the implementation of an across-the-board structural adjustment programme in the way the economy is run before any assistance can be provided. Typically, the country will be required to implement some or all of a range of measures including:

- taking fiscal measures that will have the effect of devaluing the national currency which in turn will result in raising the cost of living for most ordinary people;
- reducing the number of public service employees which will usually increase the already high unemployment level;
- cutbacks in social service spending which will affect such vital services as education and health.[17]

Transforming such developing economies from a state of economic dependency would require the taking of bold root and branch measures by a government determined to address the problems facing the country. The measures that will effectively address the problems will require that the problems be given high priority in the legislative programme.

(b) The anticipated social impact of the proposed legislation

From one point of view, the purpose of a proposed legislation may be to ameliorate an underlying social problem. From another point of view, the effect of the same legislation would be that it benefits some people and not others. A cost–benefit analysis of the proposed legislation may show that the law will impact in different ways on different sections of society. In this case, it will become apparent that there cannot be one single solution that will fit equally across the board and therefore the situation calls for a positive direct government intervention rather than relying on a market-driven solution or individual good sense.

The choice may therefore be to prioritise in favour of laws relating to improving the living conditions and quality of life of the poor majority through, for instance, increased industrialisation and consequently the creation of jobs.

---

[15]For a snippet of a not uncommon manipulative practice that will often compound the debt burden of a developing countries see Karl Maier, *This House Has Fallen: Midnight in Nigeria* (PublicAffairs, New York 2000) xxii.
[16]For a compelling description of the new world of globalisation and what it means to poor developing countries, see Noreena Hertz, *The Silent Takeover: Global Capitalism and the Death of Democracy* (Heinemann, London 2001) 1–48, 80–113.
[17]See Seidman et al (n 10) 59.

(c) The practicability of the proposed legislation, having regard to the available resources both financial and human

Clearly, there would be no sense in giving high priority to a bill intended to implement a project for which the government does not have the money or the trained human capacity. It would help to bear in mind that there are lurking in the legislative process a range of forces, some favourable, some unfavourable that the implementation of the project will encounter and there is no guarantee that the project will prevail against all the odds. Having an eye on the parliamentary timetable to get a feel of the nature and volume of business before parliament would help to assess the chances of a draft bill being included in the business for a particular session of parliament. It would therefore be wiser to make the best use of the resources that are known to be available

(d) An assessment of available drafting resources and the strains that a particular drafting request is likely to impose on them

When all the other criteria have been met, it would be important to take into account that the drafting establishment on which rests the burden of drafting the legislation has limited endurance capacity. It would help to remember that the physical strain on the drafting staff could reach a point beyond which they simply cannot operate efficiently or effectively. The public at large, and sometimes even instructing departments, are not always aware of the hard grind the drafter has to endure – the concentration of thought, the anxiety whether a relevant field implicit in the instructions has been covered in the draft, the striving for simplicity, precision and economy of language, all experienced over long and erratic hours of toil – which relentlessly imposes a mental, nervous, and physical strain on a drafter and renders the calling of a drafter a uniquely demanding profession. The nature of the drafter's calling forces the drafter to learn to do without sleep and yet remain constantly alert.[18]

In most jurisdictions the resources available, both financial and human, to do this work lag behind the demand for their services. Consequently, the need to economise and to be selective constitute powerful reason to prioritise. It stands to reason that the prioritising agency, whether centralised or departmental, would be able to prioritise effectively only if it is in possession of information regarding the current workload of the drafting establishment, the number of drafters available and an estimate of the length of person hours required to complete the drafting of the legislation that is being requested.

Conclusion

Whether or not a government succeeds in pushing through its legislative programme during its tenure will depend on a variety of factors. Some of these

---

[18] See 'Law-makers and their Instructions to Parliamentary Counsel' by the Hon. Andrew Wells QC, former Solicitor General and Judge of the Supreme Court of South Australia, contributing article in *Essays on Legislative Drafting in honour of JQ Ewens, former First Parliamentary Counsel of Australia* (Adelaide Law Review Association, Law School University of Adelaide 1988) at 126.

factors may be under the government's control and others may be beyond its control. A strong government that has an efficient political and administrative machine behind it will probably succeed where a less well organised government may not. Anyone who has knowledge of legislative drafting will confirm that the drafter is by no means a completely free agent in respect of the manner in which to carry out the task of drafting. George Bernard Shaw is reputed to have once said that every profession is a conspiracy against the public. An ill-informed critic of the variety that takes a special satisfaction in caricaturing the drafter may be forgiven for saying that Shaw's pithy statement applies to lawyers and more particularly to the drafter.

When it comes to legislative drafting, the ill-informed critic is obviously not aware of the many obstacles that stand in the way of the drafter's ability to draft freely. Priorities, largely political, play a special role and have a marked effect on the form of legislation, a fact that many of the critics who engage in the popular game of caricaturing the drafter do not understand. Of necessity, there is a political angle to what the drafter does and the reason for this is that the legislative programme of a government lies at the heart of the government's domestic activities. Bills are political instruments as well as legal instruments.

Most government Ministers are continually engaged in formulating policy to be embodied in legislation and in securing the enactment of the legislation. They therefore have a substantial interest in ensuring that the products of the legislative process give effect to the policies they have devised. Unfortunately, the picture that often emerges does not always show any of the undercurrents, such as the problem of reconciling some of the hobby-horses of Ministers and their advisers with the needs of good law making that responds to the real needs of the majority of the people. Nor does the picture always show the extent of the distortions that are sometimes created by the political rivalry between the government and the opposition parties, especially where there is a strong opposition, or even between Ministers.

It remains the job of the government to govern but it must govern creatively and judiciously. It must do so in accordance with the principles of good governance, especially through the exercise of its executive powers. In other words, it must legislate for good governance. Often this involves making difficult choices, including making use of available resources to create an atmosphere in which the generality of the population can meaningfully participate in the development of society, rather than using those resources for narrow or party political ends. Considered against this background, prioritising good governance legislation becomes an imperative rather than a matter determined by political philosophy or ideology.

Notes on contributor

Mr Richard C. Nzerem is the Hon. Director of the Sir William Dale Centre for Legislative Studies, Institute of Advanced Legal Studies of the University of London. He is also a legal consultant and former Director of the Legal and Constitutional Affairs Division, Commonwealth Secretariat. He holds an LLM (Lond).

Keeping the statute book up to date: a personal view

Duncan Berry

Consultant Parliamentary Counsel, Irish Office of the Parliamentary Counsel to the Government

From the perspective of both the state and its citizens, it is vital that up-to-date versions of legislation relevant to an issue that concerns them are capable of being identified and accessed. If legislation is not readily and immediately accessible, finding it will prove to be a task that is beyond not only lay people but also competent and experienced lawyers. A principal cause of the difficulty encountered by users of statutes and statutory rules in finding the law on a particular topic that concerns them is that often the relevant provisions are to be found not in one self-contained statute, but in a number of provisions scattered among a number of separate annual volumes. This article provides an overview of some historical and recent developments in the UK, Australia, New Zealand, Ireland, Jersey, and Canada, before proceeding to consider approaches by which responsible authorities keep their Statute Books accessible and coherent. It examines in detail the relative merits and demerits of the textual (or direct) method and the non-textual (or indirect) methods of amendment. The article concludes that the benefits of having an up-to-date, accessible and coherent Statute Book must surely be obvious. Apart from the removal of the frustration, the cost savings to both the state and the private citizen in both time and effort are surely immense.

Introduction

Since legislation incorporates the norms by which society operates, its availability in an up-to-date, accessible and coherent form is crucial for the orderly and effective functioning of society and in particular for the rule of law. From the perspective of both the state and its citizens, it is vital that up-to-date versions of legislation relevant to an issue that concerns them are capable of being identified and accessed. If legislation is not readily and immediately accessible, finding it will prove to be a task that is beyond not only lay people but also competent and experienced lawyers.

Ideally, legislation should be published in a manner that will facilitate its being identified and located by members of the public. Ensuring this outcome should be relatively straightforward. Unfortunately, this is by no means always the case, as I shall try to show in this article.

An initial problem faced by someone searching for the relevant law on a particular topic is that it is not necessarily to be found in one Act. In many cases, the relevant provisions are scattered among a number of statutes and statutory rules[1] and, quite probably, judicial decisions.

In most common law countries, the practice has been to publish statutes and statutory rules in annual volumes. Normally, each volume will consist of public general Acts arranged in the order of enactment, with any private Acts being included separately at the end of the volume. The volumes are not updated or revised, although in some common law countries it has been the practice to issue annual publications containing annotations setting out amendments to earlier statutes. Statutes that are repealed, become spent, or otherwise lose their force, are not excised. Unless there is a mechanism for revising and republishing amended statutes,[2] users of those statutes are faced with considerable difficulty in finding out what legislative provisions are relevant to them. Moreover, having found what may appear to be the provisions that concern them, they cannot rest on their laurels. They still have to check to see whether, and to what extent, those provisions have been affected by subsequent legislation and judicial decisions.

If legislation is not kept up to date, the task of researching it is unnecessarily difficult and mentally demanding, and requires much time, resources and enthusiasm. The problem is alleviated in those jurisdictions where indexes and annotations of statutes are still maintained. And in recent years, the publication in most common law jurisdictions of electronic versions of statutes and statutory rules has also made it easier to access legislation.[3]

Some historical and recent developments

The position in the United Kingdom

Some of the statutes in the United Kingdom Statute Book go back as far as the thirteenth century. The fact that many of the older ones are written in an archaic style of English make them hard to understand. Even if consolidators are able to give meaning to those statutes, they are still faced with the difficulty of translating them into modern English. Moreover, United Kingdom statutes are now overlain with large tracts of European Union law, which frequently qualifies what on the face of them might otherwise be seen to be intelligible statutes.[4]

The state of the English Statute Book attracted criticism as early as 1551. In that year King Edward VI, then only 14 years of age and a very precocious youth, wrote as follows:[5]

> I have shewed my opinion heretofore what statutes I think most necessary to be enacted this session. Nevertheless, I would wish that beside them hereafter, when time shall serve, the superfluous and tedious statutes were brought into one sum

[1]Statutory rules usually take the form of regulations, rules, bylaws or ministerial orders. In the United Kingdom and Ireland, they are called statutory instruments. Other terms used to describe this form of legislation are 'subordinate legislation', 'subsidiary legislation' and 'delegated legislation'.

[2]Along the lines of the British *Statutes Revised* or *Statutes in Force.*

[3]By means of word and phrase searches of the text.

[4]A similar situation exists in Ireland.

[5]Discourse on the Reformation of Abuses.

> together, and made more plain and short, to the intent that men might better understand them; which thing shall much help to advance the profit of the Commonwealth.

In a speech from the throne in 1609, King James I spoke of

> divers cross and cuffing statutes, and some so penned that they may be taken in divers, yea, contrary senses ... and therefore would I wish both these statutes and reports, as well in the Parliament as common law, to be once maturely reviewed and reconciled; and that not only all contrarieties should be scraped out of our bookes, but even that such penal statutes as were made but for the use of the time (from breach whereof no man can be free) which do not now agree with the condition of this our time, might likewise be left out of our bookes, which under a tyrannous or avaricious king could not be endured.

In 1616, Sir Francis Bacon, then Attorney-General to King James I, submitted to the King a proposition 'touching the compiling and amendment of the laws of England'. He proposed that the work to be done should consist of two parts. One would comprise a digest or compilation of the common laws. The other would reform and recompile the statutes. Among the reforms he envisaged was the reduction 'of statutes *heaped one upon another to one clear and uniform law*'.[6] But despite his efforts, nothing seems to have come of them. After the restoration of the monarchy in 1660, the topic was raised again, but nothing came of it. It was another 130 years before the topic resurfaced. In 1796, two reports, presented by the committees of the House of Commons, drew attention to the unsatisfactory state of the Statute Book. This led to an improvement in the classification of statutes, and to the distinction now recognised by us between public general Acts, local and personal Acts and private Acts. However, in 1800, the UK Parliament passed resolutions that led to the appointment of the First Commission on Public Records. It was under the authority of this Commission that the edition of the statutes known as the *Statutes of the Realm* was prepared. A further attempt at reform was made in 1833 with the appointment of a royal commission to codify the criminal law and to ascertain how far it might be expedient to consolidate the other branches of the law then existing in England. However, the project was over-ambitious and so yielded only limited success.

Since then the situation has improved appreciably, in that commercial publishers, such as Butterworths, produce very accurate edited versions of the Statute Book. An official electronic statute law database is now available, which contains the Scottish statutes as well as those of the United Kingdom as a whole. This is accessible by members of the general public and allows them not only to find out what the current law is but also to find out what the law was on a given date. *Halsbury's Statutes of England and Wales*, published by Butterworths, contains the primary legislation of England and Wales, with statutes being grouped under an alphabetically arranged title headings. Each statute is annotated with useful cross-references, relevant cases and subordinate legislation. *Halsbury's Statutory Instruments*, another Butterworths publication, is also arranged according to titles listed alphabetically. This publication provides up-to-date information about statutory instruments by either printing them in full with annotations, or providing a

[6]Which is symptomatic of non-textual amendments.

summary of the relevant instruments. These publications provide the equivalent of a continuously revised Statute Book (though not for Scotland or Northern Ireland). Apart from LexisNexis, there is also *Westlaw UK*, which unlike Butterworths includes Scottish material. It also includes analytical annotations. There are also other commercial publications for particular specialities. These commercial publications are the only fully updated source of information for members of the general public, but from the point of view of the general public, the disadvantage is that they charge users for access.

An official electronic *Statute Law Database* is available on the Office of Public Sector Information (OPSI) website. Legislation on this website (which also contains the Scottish statutes as well as those of the United Kingdom as a whole) is available as enacted in its original format and as revised text. Information about legislation published within the preceding two weeks and about Acts awaiting Royal Assent are to be found on the *new legislation* page of the website. The database is accessible by members of the general public and allows them not only to find out what the current law on a matter is but also to find out what the law was on a given date. The problem with the official *Statute Law Database* is that it is not up to date. The problem is exemplified by the circumstances surrounding the recent decision in *R v Chambers*.[7] I am sure most of us[8] are aware of the maxim 'ignorance of the law is no excuse' and that everyone is presumed to know the law that governs their daily activities. But people can only know what that law is if they can readily find it. With the advent of the UK *Statute Law Database*, one would have expected that in twenty-first century Britain it would not be too difficult to find out what the law is on a given point. However, as the recent decision in *Chambers*[9] illustrates, the position remains far from satisfactory. This case involved an order confiscating the profits made by Chambers from fraudulent conduct in respect of which he had been previously convicted. However, just before the Court of Appeal was about to hear an appeal against an earlier decision making a confiscation order against the appellant (Chambers), it was discovered that the regulations under which the order was to be made had been revoked as long ago as 2001.[10] No one involved in the case (including the lawyers, the judge who made the original decision, or the three appeal judges) had previously been aware that the relevant Regulations were no longer valid. At the hearing of the appeal, Lord Justice Toulson, who delivered the judgment of the Court of Appeal, was highly critical of the state of affairs. In giving judgment in the case, he had this to say:

> This case also provides an example of a wider problem. It is a maxim that ignorance of the law is no excuse, but *it is profoundly unsatisfactory if the law itself is not practically accessible*.[11] To a worryingly large extent, statutory law is not practically accessible today, even to the courts whose constitutional duty it is to interpret and enforce it. There are four principal reasons:

---

[7]All England Official Transcripts (1997–2008).
[8]Or at least those of us who are lawyers!
[9]See n 7 above.
[10]The Regulations in question were the *Excise Goods Regulations 1992*. In 2001, these Regulations were revoked and replaced by the *Tobacco Product Regulations 2001*, which are materially different from the 1992 Regulations.
[11]Emphasis added.

> First, the majority of legislation is secondary legislation.
>
> Secondly, the volume of legislation has increased very greatly over the last 40 years. The Law Commission's Report on *Post-Legislative Scrutiny*, (2006) Law Com 302, gave some figures in Appendix C. In 2005, there were 2868 pages of new Public General Acts and approximately 13,000 pages of new Statutory Instruments, making a total well in excess of 15,000 pages (which is equivalent to over 300 pages a week) excluding European Directives and European Regulations, which were responsible for over 5,000 additional pages of legislation.
>
> Thirdly, on many subjects the legislation cannot be found in a single place, but in a patchwork of primary and secondary legislation.[12]
>
> Fourthly, there is no comprehensive statute law database with hyperlinks which would enable an intelligent person, by using a search engine, to find out all the legislation on a particular topic. This means that the courts are in many cases unable to discover what the law is, or was at the date with which the court is concerned, and are entirely dependent on the parties for being able to inform them what were the relevant statutory provisions which the court has to apply. This lamentable state of affairs has been raised by responsible bodies on many occasions, including the House of Lords Committee on the *Merits of Secondary Legislation*.

As pointed out in the concluding words of Lord Justice Toulson's judgment, it is indeed a serious state of affairs when the relevant legislation is not accessible, the Government's own public information website (OPSI) is incomplete and the prosecution unintentionally misleads the court as to the relevant Regulations in force. Although the problem in the Chambers case arose in an excise context, it is symptomatic of a wider problem of significant constitutional importance.

Even though the OPSI website contains free and complete text of all statutes and statutory instruments passed or made, it would, given the amount of referential legislation that is currently on the United Kingdom statute book, be extraordinarily difficult, if not impossible, to construct a usable text of the 'as-amended legislation' from that material.

The position in Australia

Victoria

The need to keep the Statute Book up to date was recognised in Australia early on. Although, the colony of Victoria was established only in 1835, a full consolidation of the colony's Statute Book was undertaken as early as 1865. Further consolidations of Victorian legislation took place in 1890, 1915, 1928 and 1958. This has meant that the Victorian Statute Book has remained in reasonable shape from the outset. Since 1958, a regular reprinting programme has ensured that individual statutes are kept up to date. For example, the *Crimes Act 1958* has been reprinted 21 times since 1958.

---

[12]Not to mention the relevant case law, if any.

New South Wales

Initially, the situation was not so good in New South Wales. The first New South Wales statute was passed in 1824. However, by 1893, the condition of the Statute Book had deteriorated to the extent that there were calls for reform. Between 1824 and 1893, except for two or three topics, no consolidation was attempted. Furthermore, amendments, partial repeals, re-enactments, implied repeals, repeals of Acts in the formula 'so much of the said Act as is inconsistent with the present Act is hereby repealed,' adoptions of Acts with provisions quite inapplicable to New South Wales, and various other methods of legislation, had been piled one upon the other, and had brought the Statute law into a condition of confusion and entanglement.[13] This gave endless trouble to the judiciary and was a daily source of irritation and expense to all classes of the community. The position was only alleviated by the occasional publication of collections of New South Wales statutes.[14]

This led to a clearing of the Statute Book of the very large number of Acts that, for various reasons, had ceased to have any effect. By using a carefully drawn saving clause, no fewer than 602 Acts were repealed by the *Revision Act of 1898*. A further 122 Acts were repealed by similar legislation passed in 1902. Subsequently, a Royal Commissioner was appointed to make proposals for the consolidation of the New South Wales Statute Book. The Commissioner reported to the State legislature in 1902. One of the aims of the consolidation was to bring the language and arrangement of Acts as far as possible into conformity with the clearer and simpler methods of modern drafting. Preambles were to be omitted, long and involved clauses cut into shorter ones, inaccuracies removed, and inconsistencies reconciled. Furthermore, all enactments on a particular branch of the law were to be arranged in as concise, clear and orderly a manner as possible, in one consolidating statute.[15] However, no amendments 'which partook of the character of legislation ought to be ventured upon, and that all amendments, however, carefully limited to the bare necessity of the consolidation, should be noted and pointed out for the information of Parliament in the memorandum which was to accompany each Bill.'[16] According to the Commissioner, it would have been far easier, would have saved much time and an infinity of trouble, and would have avoided a great deal of risk, to repeat the clauses of the Act practically as they stood with their inaccuracies and inconsistencies. This in fact was the approach adopted in Victoria. However, in New South Wales, it was from the outset thought that a more thorough consolidation, with its great accompanying reduction in the bulk of the Statute Book, was desirable. In the event, this was accomplished.

---

[13]A sure sign that the non-textual method had been used to amend statutes.

[14]See the report of the Royal Commissioner, Charles Heydon, on Statute Law Consolidation, which was published by the New South Wales Legislative Assembly on 22 July 1902. Some official volumes of *Statutes of Practical Utility* were prepared during the period between 1900 and 1914. In all, some 14 volumes were published concurrently with the annual volumes of 'Acts as passed'.

[15]Which all sounds very modern!

[16]Ibid: see note 14.

It should be noted that the New South Wales legal profession considered the consolidation to be an inconvenience![17] Members of the profession were apparently content with a confused jumble of Acts with which they had become familiar and which they had carefully noted up with decided cases. However, every consolidation will cause this kind of inconvenience. According to the Commissioner, the preparation of a new edition of the statutes, with all the consolidations and a good index, would go a long way to remove the difficulty, which in a short time would entirely disappear.

Not long afterwards, the New South Wales legislature enacted the *Amendments Incorporation Act 1906*. That Act specifically (and I would argue significantly) for the first time authorised the reprinting of New South Wales Acts with the textual amendments[18] that had been made to them by other Acts. This Act remained in force until it was replaced by the *Reprints Act 1972*.[19] Since 1906, non-textual amendments to New South Wales statutes have been extremely rare, being confined to savings and transitional provisions and some referential amendments of a global nature. But now even savings and transitional provisions that are consequent on the enactment of amending Acts are drafted as textual amendments to the relevant principal Act.

A full consolidation of the New South Wales Statute Book was carried out in 1937.[20] In 1957, a further full consolidation was undertaken.[21] Although the volumes comprising this consolidation were prepared under the auspices of the Law Book Company, they were published with official approval. Some interest was shown in undertaking a further revision in 1977, but in the event it was decided to enhance the official reprints system rather than having a static set of bound volumes that would soon become out of date.

The reprinting of New South Wales Acts is now governed by Part 6A of the *Interpretation Act 1987* (comprising sections 45B to 45E). Section 45C of that Act now requires the New South Wales Parliamentary Counsel to compile and maintain a legislation database, which is to be published on the New South Wales legislation website. Section 45D of that Act also empowers the New South Wales Parliamentary Counsel to publish paper reprints of legislation that has been directly[22] amended. Paper reprints are now only distributed to about 100 subscribers. The New South Wales Parliamentary Counsel Office publishes paper reprints on selected titles[23] but Acts and statutory rules reprinted in paper form are of course only up to date at the time when the reprinting was completed. Under the now repealed *Reprints Act 1972*, a number of different kinds of amendments were authorised. However, apart from some very minor matters specified in section 45E of that Act, the paper reprint process is not used to make any changes to the text.

---

[17] Also see comments of Sir Courtenay Ilbert, *Mechanics of Law Making* (Clarendon Press, Oxford 1901), at 40 regarding the resistance to change of Government officials.
[18] Textual and non-textual amendments are considered in more detail below.
[19] This was originally called the *Acts Reprinting Act 1972*. This Act has now been repealed. It has been replaced by Part 6A of the *Interpretation Act 1987* (NSW).
[20] These were known colloquially as 'the Green Statutes'.
[21] And these were known colloquially as 'the Red Statutes'.
[22] Ie textually amended by inserting, omitting, varying or substituting matter.
[23] About 10,000 pages of legislation a year are reprinted in paper form.

All updating of Acts is now carried out by ordinary amending Acts, one of which is the bi-annual Statute Law Revision (Amendment) Bill.

The paper reprints system, which was formerly provided for under the *Reprints Act 1972*, has in effect been superseded by the legislation database published on the New South Wales legislation website.[24] This website has official status and covers all Acts and statutory rules. If any Act or statutory rules is amended, an up-to-date version of the Act or statutory rules is available on the official website no later than three days after the amendment has taken effect.

Queensland

In Queensland, a continuous interest had been shown in keeping the Queensland Statute Book in a clear and orderly state. Sir Samuel Griffiths[25] apparently did valuable work in the way of codifying and consolidating the Statute Book. In 1908, the Queensland legislature passed the *Statute Law Revision Act*, which authorised the publication of Acts as amended by any subsequent enactments. That Act made it clear that it was not necessary to reprint the amending Act.

Before 1 June 1992, Queensland Acts were consolidated and individually reprinted. On that date, the *Reprints Act 1992* came into force and Queensland legislation became subject to a new reprint regimen. The object of the Act is to facilitate the updating and ready availability of Queensland legislation. The Act includes extensive reprinting powers of an editorial nature, although not all of the powers are exercised in the case of every reprinted Act. The Queensland Office of the Parliamentary Counsel maintains a database of Acts in force; Acts as passed; Bills; subordinate legislation as made; and repealed legislation. This enables member of the Queensland public to have ready access to the current statute law. The database is to be found at http://www.legislation.qld.gov.au/OQPChome.htm.

South Australia

The position in South Australia was that, until the 1920s, that State's amending legislation consisted of a hotchpotch of textual and non-textual amendments.[26] A major consolidation of South Australian statutes took place in 1936, by which time the use of the textual amendment method had become the norm. In 1934, the South Australian legislature passed an *Acts Republication Act*. As one would expect from the title, this authorised the publication of amended Acts. A further full consolidation of the South Australian Statute Book was undertaken in 1976. Since all legislation is now kept on an electronic database, it is now the practice in that State to publish amended Acts to coincide with the commencement of the relevant amendments. The website is to be found at http://www.legislation.sa.gov.au. A

---

[24]<http://www.legislation.nsw.gov.au>.

[25]Who was to become the first Chief Justice of Australia after Australia became a federation on 1 January 1901.

[26]For a discussion of the relative merits of the textual and non-textual methods of amendment, see below.

visitor to the site is able to download not only the current statutory text but also historical versions of the statutory text. This greatly facilitates research.

Tasmania

In Tasmania, the *Amendments Incorporation Act 1906* authorised the publication of amended Acts. However, even before 1906, some Acts were reprinted, but they were a compilation of principal Acts and amending Acts, with no attempt being made to incorporate the amendments. From 1906 to 1997, reprinted Acts incorporating amendments to them were published periodically by the Tasmanian Government Printer. In 1997 a database of Tasmanian Legislation in electronic form was established. The database contains principal and subordinate legislation as passed by Parliament or notified in the Government Gazette and up-to-date consolidations of principal and subordinate legislation. The Tasmanian Legislation website gives free public access to up-to-date Tasmanian legislation. Hard copy reprints are available from the Tasmanian Government Printer. As is the case with most of the other States, a reprinted Act has evidentiary value but is not conclusive as to the actual state of the law in question.

Western Australia

In Western Australia, the earliest Act authorising the reprinting and publication of amended Acts was the *Statutes Compilation Act 1905*.[27] However, Acts as amended were being reprinted in a consolidated form even before the passing of the 1905 Act. In moving the second reading of the Bill that led to that Act, the Minister commented that:

> In this State, we have adopted a procedure which will be found in the Justices Act, the Criminal Code, the Electoral Act, and a number of more recent statutes. The Government Printer, in printing subsequent copies of any statute that has been amended, is entitled to embody the amendments.[28]

Later, in 1923 the *Amendments Incorporation Act 1923* was passed. The Minister moving the second reading described the Bill as a measure that 'will make for the automatic consolidation of statutes'.[29] Section 2(1) of the Act provided that:

---

[27]Section 2 of that Act provided:

> From and after the passing of this Act, whenever both Houses of the Parliament shall, by resolution, direct the compilation, with its amendments, of any Act in force in the State, it shall be the duty of the Attorney General … to prepare a compilation embodying all the provisions of such Act and the amendments thereof, omitting all those portions of the text of such Act which have been repealed or altered by subsequent Acts, and inserting in the proper places all words or sections substituted for or added to the text of the original Act by such subsequent Acts…

Section 3 required a compilation to be tabled before both Houses of Parliament.

[28]Western Australia Parliamentary Debates, 1905, 146.

[29]Western Australia Parliamentary Debates, 1923, 627.

> When any Act has … been amended … then in every reprint of the Act by the Government Printer the Act shall be printed as so amended, under the supervision of the Clerk of the Parliaments.

The 1923 Act did not repeal the 1905 Act, but instead co-existed with it. The two Acts appear to provide different means of achieving the same end. However, the Minister who moved the second reading of the 1923 Act saw a distinction, saying 'but there is also a great difference between the Act he has quoted [*Statutes Compilation Act 1905*] and the Bill before the House. The latter is merely for reprints, while the former refers to any consolidation.'

The 1923 Act was repealed by the *Amendments Incorporation Act 1938*, while the *Statutes Compilation Act 1905* remained in place until its repeal by the *Reprints Act 1984*, which is the Western Australian Act that currently authorises the publication of amended statutes. Under that Act, reprints are prepared by the Western Australian Parliamentary Counsel Office and published and sold by the State Law Publisher. In recent years, the demand for reprints has lessened because all Western Australian statutes and statutory rules are now available electronically in an up-to-date form on a website maintained by the State Law Publisher.[30] However, the Parliamentary Counsel Office still maintains a comprehensive reprinting programme that has the flow-on effect of improving the reliability of the electronic database.

The Western Australian Parliamentary Counsel Office recently completed[31] the task of capturing all of the year-by-year statutes of the State of Western Australia and the colony that preceded it in electronic form. This should prove to be a boon for people wishing to research the Western Australian statute book.

Australian Commonwealth

The Commonwealth of Australia was established on 1 January 1901. One of the earliest amending Acts enacted by the Commonwealth Parliament was the *Commonwealth Franchise Act 1902*. This was a non-textual amendment. The following year saw the first use of the textual amendment method.[32] In 1904, The *Defence Act 1904* (an amending Act) required that all amendments of the *Defence Act 1903* be incorporated in any future reprints of the principal Act. This provision was a precursor to the *Amendments Incorporation Act 1905*, which applied the same principle to all Acts and also required reprinted Acts to include notes.

In 1913, the Commonwealth published a reprint of all Commonwealth Acts in force on 1 January 1912, except Appropriation and Supply Acts. The publication included an index of all the Acts, and a table showing Acts enacted under the various provisions of the Australian Constitution. The *Statute Law Revision Act 1934* was the first general revision of Commonwealth statutes. The Act 'tidied up' the Commonwealth Statute Book in preparation for a general reprint of Commonwealth Acts.

---

[30] <http://www.slp.wa.gov.au>.

[31] This task was done entirely in-house.

[32] The *Electoral Divisions Act 1903* textually amended section 19 of the Commonwealth *Electoral Act 1902*. For a discussion of the relative merits of the textual and non-textual methods of amendment, see below.

In 1936, the Commonwealth published a reprint of all Commonwealth Acts in force 'as at 1 January 1936'. The reprint was in four volumes, with the fourth volume being an index. The first three volumes contained 2959 pages. Further volumes containing reprints of amended Commonwealth Acts were published in 1952 and 1974. In 1958, the Commonwealth published a reprint of all regulations in force as at 31 December 1956.[33] Since then, the Commonwealth has adopted the 'rolling reprint' approach, which involves reprinting Acts when they are amended and providing loose-leaf binders in which to store them.[34]

In more recent times, the Commonwealth Attorney-General's Department has established a fully up-to-date information retrieval system called *ComLaw*. *ComLaw* is an integral part of the Australian Law Online initiative to bring low or no-cost access to the law for the Australian public. *ComLaw* contains:

- Commonwealth primary legislation, as well as other ancillary documents and information, in electronic form, and
- The Federal Register of Legislative Instruments (FRLI), which that was established on 1 January 2005 under the *Legislative Instruments Act 2003* as the authoritative source for legislative instruments and compilations of legislative instruments.

As new, up-to-date compilations are added to *ComLaw* and the FRLI, the previous compilations are retained as *historical data*. If a user wants to see an item of legislation as it was in force on a particular date, this can be found in the *historical data*. The *historical data* also includes legislation of the Commonwealth that is no longer in force. The fact that principal Commonwealth statutes and statutory rules are amended only by the textual method facilitates the instant electronic consolidation of those statutes and statutory rules. The upshot is that all members of the Australian public can gain immediate access, free of charge, to the up-to-date versions of all Commonwealth statutes and statutory rules in which they are interested.

Northern Territory

Subsequent to its separation from South Australia in 1911, the Northern Territory of Australia became self-governing and was empowered to enact Ordinances for the governance of that Territory. In 1960, the Territory's Ordinances (covering the period 1911–1960) were consolidated. The consolidation was carried out under the *Amendments Incorporation Ordinance 1938–1961*. Since then, while some individual Northern Territory laws have from time to time been reprinted in individual pamphlet reprints, the Territory's laws have not been further reprinted in a consolidated form. In 1974, the Legislative Council was replaced by a fully-elected Legislative Assembly, which is empowered to enact Acts rather than Ordinances.

Electronic forms of legislation were introduced as early as the late 1970s. Up-to-date versions of Northern Territory legislation are now to be found in the

[33] There had not been a reprint of Regulations for almost 30 years.

[34] This is similar to the approach previously adopted in Victoria and subsequently in most other Australian States and Territories.

Current Northern Territory Database.[35] This database contains all the current consolidated Acts and subordinate legislation of the Northern Territory.

Each consolidated document contains amendments made to the original document that are in force. Amendments that have been made, but are not in force, are not included. The date on which a consolidated document is shown as being in force is the date on which the last amendment of the document came into force.

Historical consolidations of Acts and subordinate legislation of the Northern Territory are available on the Northern Territory Legislation History Database. Bills introduced in the Legislative Assembly, and numbered Acts and subordinate legislation of the Northern Territory, are available on the Register of Legislation Database.

All of the databases are also available on the Hansard & Legislation page of the Northern Territory Government website at <http://www.nt.gov.au/lant/hansard/hansard.shtml>.

Amendments continue to be included in a reprint under the *Amendments Incorporation Act* and the timeline for this process is no later than two weeks after an amendment commences. To facilitate the production of up-to-date versions of principal Acts, amendments are made textually.

Australia as a Whole

In addition to the legislation databases established by the Australian Commonwealth and the various States and Territories of Australia, the Australasian Legal Information Institute (AustLII) provides free internet access to Australasian legal information (including primary and secondary legislation). AustLII's broad public policy agenda is to improve access to justice through better access to legal information. AustLII has become one of the largest sources of legal texts on the Internet, with over 20 gigabytes of raw text materials and over 4 million searchable documents.[36]

The position in New Zealand

New Zealand departed from the English form of statutes at a very early date.[37] One major departure was the inclusion of an 'Analysis' (in effect a table of contents). It was many years before this useful practice was adopted in Australia. The textual method of amendment was adopted at an earlier date, although non-textual 'stand-alone' amending Acts were enacted on rare occasions.[38]

---

[35]For the Northern Territory legislative database, see: <http://www.dcm.nt.gov.au/strong_service_delivery/supporting_government/current_northern_territory_legislation_database>.

[36]Similar databases are to be found in other jurisdictions. For example, in Hong Kong, the Hong Kong Legal Information Institute (HKLII), a project of Law & Technology Centre (a centre jointly established by Department of Computer Science and Faculty of Law of the University of Hong Kong), provides the public with legal information relating to Hong Kong. Similarly, the British and Irish Legal Information Institute (BAILII) operates a publicly accessible data base containing British and Irish case law and legislation, European Union case law, Law Commission reports, and other law-related British and Irish materals.'

[37]See Walter Iles, 'Legislative Drafting Practices in New Zealand' (1992) Statute Law Review 16–30.

[38]Eg The Fisheries Amendment Act 1963.

In 1908, a full revision of New Zealand statutes was undertaken. Consequently, it is almost unheard of to have to look for a New Zealand statute enacted earlier than that year. The first general reprint of the Public Acts was undertaken in 1931. A further general reprint of Public Acts began in 1957. The reprints were authorised by the *Statutes Drafting and Compilation Act 1920* (still in force in 2005). Reprinted versions of statutory regulations have been published under the authority of the *Regulations Act 1936*.

After 1957, statutes were reprinted individually and published as part of the annual volumes for each year. Reprints of regulations were done only occasionally.[39] This approach to reprinting statutes continued until 1979 when the *Reprinted Statutes of New Zealand* series commenced. This series[40] comprised bound volumes of reprinted statutes published annually. Individual reprinted Acts were also available in pamphlet form. The intention was to reprint progressively all statutes on the New Zealand statute book to the point where every public Act of general application would be available in a form that was not more than 10 years old, but with Acts in common use or those that had been heavily amended being reprinted more regularly. This system continued until 2003 when it ceased and was replaced by the reprinting of individual statutes in pamphlet form only. This has enabled a significantly greater number of reprints to be compiled and published. Reprints are published using the reprint powers in the Acts and *Regulations Publication Act 1989*, which allows the reprinted statutes to be published in the format and style adopted for New Zealand legislation in 2000 and to reflect current drafting practice. Statutes and statutory rules are reprinted in accordance with a reprints policy and an annual reprints programme that are designed to ensure that reprinting meets demand. Extensive consultation is undertaken each year to determine which statutes and statutory rules are to be reprinted.

The *Legislative Enactments of New Zealand* (LENZ) enables up-to-date versions of statutes and statutory rules to be made available to the public free via the internet. The system (formerly known as the *Public Access to Legislation* (PAL system)) is an integrated drafting and publishing system that allows legislation to be made available in printed and electronic form from a database owned and maintained by the New Zealand Government. The database is in the process of being 'officialised', that is, checked for accuracy and made consistent with current format and drafting practice with a view to the electronic version becoming authoritative in the same way as hard copy. It is also intended to use the system to produce prospective consolidations, that is, versions of how a statute will look with proposed amendments incorporated into it. Bills at all stages of the parliamentary process are also available on-line.

The position in Ireland

Although no general revision of the Statute Book has yet taken place in Ireland, as mentioned elsewhere, some major statutes have been consolidated in recent years and, since the millennium, it has become the practice to use the textual method for amending statutes. Apart from the *Social Welfare (Consolidation) Act 1981*, the

[39] Eg Electoral Regulations prior to a general election

[40] Referred to by some as the 'Brown Volumes'.

Social Welfare (Consolidation) Act 1993, the *Taxes Consolidation Act 1997* and the *Stamp Duties Consolidation Act 1999*, there have very been few consolidations of Irish statute law in recent years. One recent exception has been the *Land and Conveyancing Law Reform Act 2009* (Ire), which provides for a comprehensive reform and modernisation of land law and conveyancing law in Ireland and is the result of a joint project undertaken by the Department of Justice, Equality and Law Reform and the Law Reform Commission. The Act repeals in whole or in part in the region of 150 pre-1922 statutes and their replacement, where appropriate, with statutory provisions more suited to modern conditions.

The *Statute Law (Restatement) Act 2002* ostensibly enables the Attorney General to authorise a statute, or portion of a statute, to be made available in printed or electronic form in the form of a single text certified to be a statement of the law contained in the provisions of the statutes to which it relates. To date, no restatements have been made under the Act. The main reason for this is that the Act is only useful for the restatement of Acts and statutory instruments that have been amended *only* by the textual method. However, most Irish principal Acts have been amended by a hotchpotch of textual and non textual amendments. So the Act can only come into its own when all non-textually amended Irish Acts and statutory instruments have been consolidated and re-enacted. Since there are no votes in undertaking such consolidations, there is unlikely to be any improvement in the Irish position in the near future. This is regrettable because, in the absence of regular consolidation, it is extraordinarily difficult to find out exactly what the law is under Irish statutes that have been amended (whether textually or non-textually).

One recent development in Ireland has been the revision of pre-1922[41] statutes. As a preliminary step to revision, a review of all pre-1922 statutes was undertaken. The upshot was the enactment of the *Statute Law Revision Act 2007*. This Act followed the examination of 26,370 pre-1922 statutes of a public and general nature. Of those Acts, 9219 were already wholly repealed and 12,562 were found not to be applicable to Ireland. This left 4589 statutes in force, of which 3225 were expressly repealed and 1364 were expressly retained by that Act. The effect of not being included in that Act was that those United Kingdom Acts that did not apply to Ireland before 1922 were implicitly repealed and thus formally ceased to be part of the Irish statute book.

In 2009, the Statute Law Revision Bill 2009 (Ire) was published. This Bill followed a review of 3182 pre-1751 Private Acts (Irish, English and United Kingdom) and 7543 pre-1851 local and personal United Kingdom Acts. Apart from those Acts already repealed, 8957 were assessed as being not applicable to Ireland. A further 138 Acts were identified as being not suitable for repeal as they were found to contain provisions that could have a continuing relevance. The remaining 1351 Acts have been assessed as suitable for express repeal.

Because the *Statute Law Revision Act 2007* (Ire) and the Statute Law Revision Bill 2009 list for the periods involved all the Acts that are not repealed, they will together provide a comprehensive list of all primary legislation still in force for those periods at the time of enactment of the 2007 Act and, when enacted, of the 2009 Bill.

However despite these developments, progress in achieving a coherent, up-to-date and accessible Irish statute book can, at best, be said to be only modest.

---

[41] 1922 was the year in which Ireland gained its independence from the United Kingdom.

The position in Jersey, Channel Islands

In 2005, a full-scale revision of statutes was completed in Jersey. As a result of the revision, it is now relatively easy for the Jersey Statute Book to be kept up to date even when statutes are extensively amended. All Jersey statutes continued to remain in force after the revision but were, for example, made gender neutral and in most cases were renumbered, with spent provisions being omitted.

The position in Canada

As early as the middle of the nineteenth century, what were then Canadian colonies recognised the need to completely update their legislation so that it would be in a form accessible to members of the public. The procedure developed for the purpose was called a 'statute revision'. In its ordinary sense, the term 'revision' means the correction and rewriting of a text that is for any reason found to be unsatisfactory. Revision in this sense is quite different from 'consolidation', which is defined and described elsewhere in this article. In the Canadian context, the term 'statute revision' has come to mean a combination of consolidation; rewriting whenever necessary; and rearranging the various statutes and their respective contents. In undertaking the revision of a statute, the revisers are usually empowered to modify the existing text, but only so long as they do not alter the substance of the law. Apart from correcting editing, grammatical, and typographical errors, the language of a statute may be altered in order 'to preserve a uniform mode of expression' as long as the substance is not changed. Changes to reconcile 'seemingly inconsistent enactments' are also allowed. If the different official language versions of a statute are incompatible, changes can be made to reconcile them. More recently, action has been taken to standardise the wording of frequently used provisions and to shortening long sections and subsections by splitting them into shorter and more readable provisions. Efforts have also been made to eradicate archaic expressions (including most Latinisms, such as *mutatis mutandis*).

At the federal level, several general revisions of the statutes of Canada have been made since Canada was established in 1867. The first was in 1886, less than 20 years after federation. Further revisions of federal statutes were undertaken in 1906, 1927, 1952, 1970 and 1985. In each case, a Statute Revision Commission was appointed under the authority of an Act of Parliament. The Commission's brief was to examine, consolidate and revise all public general statutes. The revised statutes were then published in a series of volumes under the title *Revised Statutes of Canada* with the addition of the year of publication. One way in which a statute revision in Canada significantly differs from a reprinted statute published in the various Australian jurisdictions is that the Acts authorising a revision of Canadian statutes provided that, after the revision was completed and the revised statutes had been deposited in the office of the Clerk of the Parliaments, they were to be brought into force by proclamation of the Governor General. The authorising Acts also provided that, on the coming into force of the revised statutes, the pre-revision versions of the statutes were to be repealed.

After the 1970 revision, a decision was taken to replace the system of appointing an ad hoc commission for each revision by establishing a permanent statute revision commission whose members and staff would be employees of the federal Department of Justice. However, those employees were required to be experienced in drafting and editing legislation. One of the principal reasons for appointing a permanent commission was to make it possible to undertake revisions of statutes on a continuing basis with a view to shortening the intervals between the years in which revised statutes were published. The Minister of Justice has recently appointed three new members of the Commission.[42] The Cabinet also brought into force new provisions of the Act (re-named the Legislation Revision and Consolidation Act) that provide for the revision of regulations (in addition to Acts) and give evidentiary force to the electronic consolidation published by the Minister of Justice.[43]

As early as 1970, a computer database of all federal legislation was established and the Act establishing the 1974 Statute Revision Commission provided not only for the continuing revision of both statutes and regulations but also for the possibility for the institution of a loose-leaf system of continuous consolidation of statutes. However, the loose-leaf system has now been abandoned since statutes and statutory rules became accessible electronically. The change to a system of continuous revision meant that it was no longer possible to repeal and replace the whole Statute Book at once.[44] The current practice is for the federal Minister for Justice to lay drafts of revised statutes before the appropriate parliamentary committee for examination and approval. After the committee has approved the revised statutes, the Minister then introduces a Bill to bring them into force.

In the early years of the Canadian federation, the Canadian provinces were rather more assiduous than federal Canada in keeping their statutes up to date. The system for revision adopted at the provincial level is similar to that used at the federal level. Thus, Ontario has undertaken a number of general revisions entitled *Revised Statutes of Ontario*, the first one being in 1877. In Quebec, the first revision was undertaken in 1888 and others have been undertaken at regular intervals since then. Similarly, the provinces of Alberta, British Columbia, Manitoba, New Brunswick, Nova Scotia, and Saskatchewan have all undertaken revisions of their statutes at regular intervals since the establishment of the Canadian federation.

British Columbia carried out a major revision in 1996. The 1992 *Statute Revision Act*[45] that authorised the 1996 general revision of British Columbia statutes separately authorised general revisions of all Public Acts and limited revisions of individual Acts or parts of Acts to allow for a different citation method between these. The 1992 Act also provided specific authority for considerable plain language redrafting that was used, given resources, for a number of key statutes. As is the case with other Canadian jurisdictions, British Columbia has never used its

---

[42]The members are John Mark Keyes (Chairperson), François LaFontaine and Ingrid Ludchen.

[43]See <http://laws.justice.gc.ca/en/>.

[44]In fact, there was never a full revision that replaced the whole Canadian federal statute book. Revisions always omitted private Acts and Acts of narrow or temporary application. All revisions (including the 1985 revision) have included all other laws. To date there has never been a selective revision of only a few Acts. Until June 2009, the computer database of Canadian federal statutes was unofficial. However, it is understood that the Department of Justice is now planning to undertake selective revisions of a group of Acts at a time.

[45]The Act is now RSBC 1996, c 440.

authority to carry out limited statute revisions, other than for Private Acts.[46] However, it is believed that the Office of Legislative Counsel in British Columbia does plan to use its limited revision powers to update major Acts, focusing on those that have been subject to significant amendment. Implementation of these plans is dependent on the availability of legislative drafting resources that are not immediately needed for the preparation of legislation that is on the Government's legislative programme. However, limited revisions will only be possible if the Government provides the funding for the resources needed to produce them. Past experience suggests that providing funds for this kind of activity has not been high on the Government's political agenda.

British Columbia has had a loose-leaf consolidation since the Revised Statutes of British Columbia 1979. This is prepared by the British Columbia Office of Legislative Counsel in conjunction with the Queen's Printer.

The province's electronic consolidation is prepared by the Queen's Printer, based on information from the on-going *Table of Legislative Changes* maintained by the Office of Legislative Counsel. However, the electronic consolidation is not official, which is probably just as well as it is not uncommon to find amendment errors that arose during the consolidation process.[47]

In recent years, the loose-leaf consolidation has fallen many months behind the electronic consolidation. This is partly because it requires much more work to ensure accuracy of the paper version and to do the publishing formatting.

Saskatchewan is currently in the process of carrying out a revision. Other Canadian provinces have ceased carrying out revisions at regular intervals. For example, Ontario has not undertaken a revision since 1990.[48] In all Canadian jurisdictions, continuing electronic consolidation has now largely supplanted paper[49] revision.

Why the Statute Book may not be up to date, accessible and coherent

A principal cause of the difficulty encountered by users of statutes and statutory rules in finding the law on a particular topic that concerns them is that often the relevant provisions are to be found not in one self-contained statute, but in a number of provisions scattered among a number of separate annual volumes. Often some of these provisions will deal with matters other than the one with which the user is concerned.

As anyone who is familiar with the Statute Book of any common law jurisdiction will be aware, the bulk of legislation amends existing legislation and it seems to me that a major source of the problem lies in the method by which statutes and statutory rules are amended. In essence, two methods are available for amending

[46]The Law Clerk of the BC Legislative Assembly will request a revision when there are amendments to a substantial Private Act.
[47]However, the Office of Legislative Counsel monitors the electronic consolidation and thus ensures that any errors that are found are promptly corrected.
[48]Ontario used to carry out statute revisions every 10 years.
[49]Ie 'hard copy'.

legislation. One method is the non-textual or indirect method. The other is the textual or direct method.[50]

A non-textual amendment does not alter the text of the old law but consists of a discursive statement or narrative of the effect of the amendment on the old law. Because the text of the law that is to be amended remains unaltered, the amendment operates indirectly. With this technique, the amending law does not merge with the Act being amended. Nor does it lose its separate identity in the Statute Book. As Thornton[51] points out, use of the method involves legislating referentially. The ultimate effect is a cumulative one as statute is piled on statute, with the result that comprehension becomes more and more difficult.

An example of a non-textual amendment is to be found in section 1 (4) of the *Infanticide Act 1949* (Ire), which states as follows:

> Section 60 of the *Offences Against the Person Act 1861* shall have effect as if the reference therein to the murder of any child included a reference to infanticide.

Another example is to be found in section 37 of the *Town and County Planning Act 1968* (UK), which non-textually amends section 149 of the *Town and County Planning Act 1962*, section 37(3) provides as follows:

> For a person to be treated under section 149 (1) or (3) of the principal Act (definitions for the purposes of blight notices provisions) as owner-occupier or resident owner-occupier of a hereditament, his occupation thereof at a relevant time or during a relevant period, if not occupation of the whole of the hereditament, must be, or, as the case may be, have been occupation of a substantial part of it.

The perceived advantage of a non-textual amendment is that it should make sense when standing alone, although that is clearly not the case with the example taken from the *Infanticide Act 1949.* The user should be able to ascertain the effect of the amendment, a matter of convenience that is claimed to be important from a legislator's perspective. One advantage that non-textual amendments can have is that of effecting, in one measure, the blanket amendment of a number of different provisions.

Non-textual amendments are often used to make global changes. For example, on a change of currency, it is necessary to convert all statutory references from the old currency to the new currency. When Ireland changed to decimal currency in 1970, this was achieved by section 9(1) of the *Decimal Currency Act 1970* (Ire) which provided a general formula for amending existing references to outmoded shillings and pence. Likewise, the *Euro Changeover (Amounts) Act 2001* (Ire) achieved the same purpose, when the euro replaced the Irish pound.[52]

An over-reliance on the use of non-textual amendments is that a set of cross-references, interpretations and qualifications develops. This adds to the complexity and lack of coherence of the Statute Book. As a result, it becomes exceedingly

---

[50] In this article, I use the term non-textual method and textual method rather than indirect method and direct method, but they more or less amount to the same thing. For a discussion of the relative merits of the textual and non-textual methods of amendment, see below.
[51] GC Thornton, *Legislative Drafting* (4th edn LexisNexis, London 1996) at 405.
[52] Arguably, the same result could have been achieved by legislation that was drafted in the form of textual amendments.

difficult (if not impossible) to collect the text of legislation on a particular topic in a single instrument. Even if an attempt is made to produce such an instrument, the result will be virtually unusable, since it will be impossible to create a unified, coherent text. For these reasons, the current view is that textual amendments are to be preferred for their relative simplicity.[53] For instance, section 1(4) of the *Infanticide Act 1949* (Ire) would have been as effective had it directly amended the text of section 60 of the *Offences Against the Person Act 1961.* A textual amendment in that case could have said: 'Section 60 of the *Offences Against the Person Act 1861* is amended by inserting "or infanticide" after "murder of any child".'

This would have been a tidier method of amendment and would have facilitated the subsequent consolidation of the 1861 Act. As it now stands, section 60 has to be read as if the words 'or infanticide' are to be implied in the section but they do not form part of its text. Thus, the Statute Books of those jurisdictions where non-textual amendments are used are a curious mixture of textual and non textual amendments. Thornton's observations on this are apposite:

> The traditional ... style, therefore, produced a pottage comprising direct amendments, indirect amendments and provisions incorporating both techniques. The effect, at least to one not nurtured from his early years on English statutes, is confusing, particularly so as it rests on a stream of consistently invidious and inevitably inconsistent decisions as to which amendments should properly be effected by one method, which by the other, and which of both.[54]

On the other hand, a textual amendment is one that amends an existing enactment or statutory rule by repealing words or provisions; by substituting new words or provisions for existing ones; or by inserting into the enactment or rule additional words or provisions. When this method is used, the problem faced by the legislator or user is that the change made to the law is not immediately intelligible. In order to understand the amendment and what it does, it is necessary for the legislator or user to read the text of the amended enactment or rule with the amendment incorporated into it. In some jurisdictions, parliamentary counsel include in their amending Bills a note showing what a provision will look like when the amendment is incorporated.[55]

However, in most jurisdictions a comprehensive explanatory note is provided so that the legislator or user can immediately see what the existing law is; what the amendment does to that law; and what effect the amendment has on the existing law. In some cases, in order to provide a complete explanation of the amendment, the explanation has to be longer than the amendment. In most legislative drafting offices, these notes are prepared by the parliamentary counsel responsible for

---

[53] Thornton, *Legislative Drafting* (n 50) 407; DR Miers and AC Page, *Legislation* (2nd edn Sweet and Maxwell, London 1990) 195–196.

[54] Thornton, *Legislative Drafting* (n 50) 406–407.

[55] In the United Kingdom, this device has been adopted on some occasions by means of what are known as Keeling Schedules. A Keeling Schedule shows, in a Schedule to the relevant Bill, how the law will look once it is amended. It is also makes it clear in the text of the Bill itself how the law is being amended. See paragraphs 13.21 and 13.22 of the Renton Report: *The Preparation of Legislation*, Report of a committee appointed by the Lord President of the Council and chaired by (then) Sir David Renton (1977).

drafting the relevant Bill.[56] But even in cases where explanatory notes are prepared by government officials, the final responsibility for their contents should[57] remain with parliamentary counsel who drafted the Bill.

In my view, the advantages of the textual amendment method greatly outweigh the non-textual method. Thornton has listed a number of them.[58] These are as follows:

- The [textual] method produces law that is simpler and easier to understand, provided that the reprints, revisions or consolidations are produced frequently.
- The [textual] method reduces the proliferation of statutes.
- To some extent, [the textual method] makes consolidation a running exercise thus facilitating the production of consolidated reprints or revisions without the need for specific legislation.
- By encouraging the integration of new and modified provisions with the old, [the textual method] encourages a view of the law on a particular subject as a whole rather than as a series of interwoven but separate parts.
- By directly integrating the new provisions with the old, [the textual method] reduces the potential for repeal by implication.
- [The textual method] facilitates annotation.
- Not least, [textual] amendments are easier to draft.

I would add two further advantages. Because textual amendments are relatively easy to incorporate into the relevant principal enactment or statutory rule, the resources involved in keeping the law up to date are much reduced. This is because the incorporations can be made by skilled clerical staff, whereas the services of experienced, specialist lawyers are required in order to prepare consolidations of laws that are a mixture of non-textual and textual amendments. Moreover, if a principal statute or statutory rule is amended only by textual amendments, it becomes unnecessary to include provisions such as the following:[59]

> This Act and the National Treasury Management Agency Act 1990 shall be construed together as one and may be cited as the National Treasury Management Agency Acts 1990 and 2000.

Tidying up the Statute Book

So how should the responsible authorities keep their Statute Books accessible and coherent? A number of approaches can be adopted. One is to enact statute law revision legislation that clears the Statute Book of deadwood. Such legislation repeals those statutes that have become obsolete and have no practical value. The usual practice is expressly to provide that the revision does not affect any existing rules

---

[56]However, in the United Kingdom and Ireland, explanatory notes are usually prepared by government officials.
[57]And in fact it usually does.
[58]Thornton, *Legislative Drafting* (n 50) 407.
[59]I have found that it is not unusual for these collective citations not to be kept up to date or for one in a series to be missed.

or principles. But statute law revision is only a partial solution as old statutes that are still in operation are left untouched. Moreover, the physical state of the Statute Book remains intact. The old statutes that have been repealed, and therefore no longer form part of the law, remain in the official volumes of statutes. The user still has to check whether a particular provision is in force or not.

Another approach is the periodic re-publication of statutes in their revised form, incorporating the amended text and purged of repealed and spent provisions. As already mentioned, this kind of approach is adopted in the Australian Commonwealth and its States and Territories. Each of those jurisdictions has special legislation that facilitates the periodic reprinting of statutes and statutory rules.[60] The process involves publishing a statute in a single updated text that takes account of all amendments that have been made to it since it was first enacted.

A reprinted Act is thus simply a means of providing an up-to-date, accessible and coherent version of existing legislation. Although the process is an administrative one, the publisher[61] is usually allowed to make certain style changes, such as changing numbers or dates from words to figures or changing long-form cross-references to short-form ones. This method not only ensures that accessible and coherent statutes and statutory rules are available to users, but it also obviates the need to take up the time of the legislature, which is at best a scarce resource. Although a reprinted statute or statutory rule does not of itself normally have the force of law, it is prima facie evidence of the law contained in the provision to which it relates.

In Australia,[62] New Zealand and Hong Kong, electronic versions of statutes are now normally publicly available within days if not hours after the amendments have taken effect. Also in Australia, pamphlet copies of updated versions of statutes and statutory rules are also published on a periodic basis. The Hong Kong Department of Justice, which produces consolidated versions of Hong Kong statutes and statutory rules in a loose-leaf system, publishes replacement pages for legislation shortly after it has been amended. In Canada, the Department of Justice publishes electronic versions of updated versions of federal statutes and regulations.[63] Up-to-date

---

[60]The *Amendments Incorporation Act 1905* requires the Australian Government Printer to publish reprinted updated versions of amended statutes and statutory rules. However, this work is now undertaken in the Office of Legislative Drafting and Publications in Canberra. In New South Wales, the *Reprints Act 1972* authorises the Parliamentary Counsel to issue updated versions of statutes and statutory rules. Similar legislation operates in Queensland (the *Reprints Act 1992*); in South Australia (the *Legislation Revision and Publication Act 2002*); in Tasmania (the *Legislation Publication Act 1996*); in Victoria (section 21A of the *Interpretation of Legislation Act 1984*); and in Western Australia (the *Reprints Act 1984*). In New Zealand, compilations of amended statutes are prepared under the *Statutes Drafting and Compilation Act 1920*. In Hong Kong, section 99 of the *Interpretation and General Clauses Ordinance* authorises the Government Printer to print copies of Ordinances with all amendments made by amending Ordinances. Such copies are treated as authentic versions of the amended Ordinances.

[61]The official designated to be the publisher will normally be the Government (or Queen's) Printer, the Attorney General or the Parliamentary Counsel.

[62]Both at the federal and state levels. For example, for compilations of Australian Commonwealth Acts, see <http://www.comlaw.gov.au/ComLaw/legislation> and for consolidated versions of New South Wales statutes and statutory rules, see <http://www.legislation.nsw.gov.au>.

[63]Eg see <http://laws.justice.gc.ca/>.

electronic versions of statutes and statutory rules of Canadian provinces are similarly available.[64]

However, the effectiveness of the reprint or compilation system as used in Australia and other Commonwealth countries is closely tied to the use of the textual method of amendment. If the public is to have access to up-to-date, accessible and coherent revised versions of amended statutes and statutory rules, it is essential that the amendments should be effected *only* by the textual method. As the Renton Report makes clear,[65] to the extent that there is a conflict between the needs of the legislator and the statute user, the needs of the user should prevail. The report goes on to say:

> Many statutes are already difficult enough to understand in themselves without making their sense even more abstruse by amending them in a manner which further perplexes the user. There is no doubt that the non-textual amendment of existing legislation often adds to the burdens of the user, particularly when the consolidation of heavily amended legislation is held up for one reason or another.

I could not agree more!

So why has use of the non-textual method been so prevalent in past amending statutes? The following extract from Sir Courtenay Ilbert's work *The Mechanics of Law Making* seems to provide the answer:[66]

> In the first place, it [i.e. an Act that textually amends another Act] is absolutely unintelligible without the text of the enactments which it is proposed to amend, and even if these objections can be removed by means of an explanatory memorandum, a bill thus drawn is, as anyone who has watched attempts to frame parliamentary amendments will readily understand, extremely difficult to amend, and thus presents unreasonable obstacles to legitimate discussion in committee. For these reasons, this technical method of amendment is hardly ever adopted in England except in the case of non-contentious measures. In these circumstances, the ordinary mode of amending an Act is to state in the amending bill the effect of the amendment proposed to be made. This is the commonest mode, and for English parliamentary purposes is the most convenient, because under it every Member of Parliament who knows anything of the subject learns at once the nature of the amendment proposed. And in some cases, where the amendment virtually overrides a large portion of the existing enactment, it is practically the only possible method.

Regrettably, this view subordinates the needs of statute users and the long-term coherence of the Statute Book to the short-term needs of parliamentarians. And, as Ilbert conceded, there are other ways of communicating the effect of proposed amendments to parliamentarians. He also expresses with approval the approach adopted in the Indian legislature. Having stated that ideally amendments should be made by repealing and replacing the whole of the section or part affected, he went on to say:

---

[64] Eg see <http://www.e-laws.gov.on.ca/DBLaws/Statutes/> for the legislation of Ontario and <http://www.qp.gov.bc.ca/statreg/default.htm> for the legislation of British Columbia.
[65] See n 54. See para 13.17 of the report.
[66] Ilbert (n 17) 129.

> [T]he next most convenient course, from the point of view of administration, is to express the amendments in a technical form, like notices of amendments to bills in Parliament, or like errata or addenda in books; that is to say, in the form of directions to strike out particular words or sentences from an enactment, and to add others. This it is the form frequently adopted by the Indian legislatures. It enables a clerk to note up, almost mechanically, the alterations in the statute law, by simple striking out or writing in the necessary words.
>
> Thanks to this method of amendment, the Legislative Department of the Government of India is able to issue periodically revised editions of the most important Indian Acts, which embody the amendments up to date, and thus, for many purposes, take the place of repealing and consolidating Acts. But for purposes of practical administration such reprints are of great convenience.

One cannot help wondering why a system that was good enough (and thought to be even desirable) for India was not considered appropriate for the United Kingdom! In my view, the approach adopted in India (probably as a result of the influence of the British jurist, Sir James Stephen) was the right one.[67] The adoption of a similar approach in Australia, Canada and New Zealand has certainly helped to ensure that each jurisdiction in those countries has a Statute Book that is up to date, accessible and coherent.[68]

Although the Renton Report favours the textual method of amendment, it nevertheless concludes that its adoption will never eliminate the need for consolidation, if only because there can be no rigid rule that amendment must always be effected textually and so there is bound to continue to be some flow of legislation having non-textual effects on earlier legislation on the same matter. However, I have to disagree with this conclusion. Even on the rare occasion when non-textual amendments are necessary,[69] this should only be regarded as a stopgap measure. I believe it should always be possible[70] to convert those amendments to textual ones shortly after the enactment containing them.

A third method for alleviating the problem is to enact consolidating legislation.[71] A consolidating Act is one that re-enacts all the relevant provisions on a particular subject in one statute, making, at most, only minor amendments to the

---

[67]Stephen served (1869–72) as the legal member of the Viceroy's Council in India, preparing a draft codification (later adopted) of the law relating to contracts, crime, and evidence. He later drafted a codification of English criminal law, but the United Kingdom Parliament never enacted it.

[68]Likewise in Hong Kong, where the Law Drafting Division of the Department of Justice maintains up-to-date sets of loose-leaf reprinted statutes and statutory rules.

[69]Such as was the case with the *Reunification Ordinance* enacted by the Hong Kong Provisional Legislative Council during the early hours of the morning of 1 July 1997 in consequence of the resumption of the sovereignty of Hong Kong by the People's Republic of China. However, the various non-textual referential amendments were later converted to textual ones by means of a systematic programme of amending legislation.

[70]Eg by means of a Statute Law (Miscellaneous Provisions) Bill.

[71]See Lord Simon of Glaisdale and JVD Webb, 'Consolidation and Statute Law Revision' (1975) PL 285.

existing law.[72] Many Parliaments in common law countries have special parliamentary procedures to expedite the enactment of such legislation. For example, in Ireland, several Acts have been passed using such procedure.[73] The *Taxes Consolidation Act 1997* (Ire) exemplifies the benefits associated with consolidation. It consolidated the law on income tax, capital gains tax and corporation tax and, in the process, reduced its bulk. Provisions that were formerly contained in 40 separate statutes are now found in a single Act, with over 2000 different sections being reduced to 1104 sections and 50 schedules being condensed to 32.[74] The consolidated Act was drafted and structured with users (principally taxation officers, taxpayers, tax practitioners and accountants) in mind. There is no doubt that the Act's more coherent format eases the task of finding the relevant Irish law on taxation. However, despite the Act having been quite extensively amended since 1997 and those amendments having been made textually, no up-to-date version of the Act is currently available.

A fourth method is to carry out statute revisions as is the practice in all Canadian jurisdictions. A revision will normally go further than a consolidation. In the Canadian parlance, 'statute revision' has come to mean a combination of consolidation, rewriting where necessary and rearranging the order in which provisions appear. As is the case with a pure consolidation or a reprint, the only modifications that are permitted are ones that do not change the substance of the statute or regulation under revision.

A fifth method is a codifying statute, which enacts in one statute all the relevant provisions on a topic, often making major changes to the existing law.[75] Common law jurisdictions have tended to be hostile to codification. But there are exceptions. Queensland, Tasmania and the Northern Territory of Australia have all codified their respective criminal laws, as has New Zealand. And in Ireland, the *Succession Act 1965* can be cited as an example of a codifying measure. These measures help to reduce the bulk and cumbersome nature of the Statute Book, but they are of limited assistance. Due to the time and effort involved in their drafting and

---

[72] Ilbert (n 17) 36 and 37, described consolidation in the following terms:

> By consolidation I mean the combination into a single statute of several statutes or parts of statutes dealing with the same subject. … Consolidation deals with statute law alone as interpreted and explained by judicial decisions. … In consolidating statute law, you have to consider and reproduce, unless you determine to alter, the effect of judicial decisions. You also have to consider the reciprocal bearing of the statute law and of the rules of common law on which it is based, which it presupposes and which it may or may not vary.

[73] Eg see the *Fisheries (Consolidation) Act 1959*, the *Income Tax Act 1967, the Social Welfare (Consolidation) Act 1981*, the *Social Welfare (Consolidation) Act 1993*, the *Taxes Consolidation Act 1997* and the *Stamp Duties Consolidation Act 1999*.

[74] L Hennessy and P Moore, *Taxes Consolidation Act 1997: the Busy Practitioner's Guide* (Institute of Taxation in Ireland, Dublin 1997) 3.

[75] Ilbert (n 17) 36 and 37 has described codification in the following terms:

> By codification I mean the reduction into a systematic form of the whole of the law, statute law or common law. … Codification deals both with common law and with statute law. … In codifying common law, you have to incorporate rules which have already been reduced to statutory form.

preparation and competing demands on the parliamentary agenda such legislation tends to be infrequent.

If a country's Statute Book is not systematically kept up to date on an ongoing basis, the task of revising it and making it accessible and coherent will be a monumental one. If the country's laws have not been consistently amended by the textual method, it will mean that the reprint method will not work and they will have to be consolidated as part of a comprehensive programme. Such a programme will involve a commitment of financial and human resources (through, for instance, the recruitment of additional legislative drafting staff) which historically Governments have been notoriously reluctant to approve. Moreover, it would require the allocation of time on the legislative agenda, at times when the Government might consider other proposals more desirable or politically important.

As part of the process, the manner in which legislation is published needs to be addressed. Legislative reform and statute law revision in itself does not reduce the actual physical bulk of the volumes of statutes that retain amended and repealed legislation. Statute users want (and need) to be provided with the up-to-date text of legislation, not to be presented with the opportunity to engage in a fascinating intellectual challenge of navigating backwards and forwards through volume after volume of statutes. The publication of legislation in its current, as well as its historical, form is crucial and to this end the production on regular basis of a revised Statute Book is desirable. The publication on a commercial basis of the loose-leaf consolidated statutes and statutory rules[76] would certainly help. And, with the advent of modern computer technology, it is now feasible (as indeed has been frequently demonstrated in Australia and Canada) to produce electronic versions of updated statutes and statutory rules within days of their being amended. And of course, electronic versions of legislation are much, much easier to search than hard copies are.

Reforming an out-of-date Statute Book: what needs to be done

On the assumption that a Statute Book has become out of date, inaccessible and jumbled, here are the measures that I believe need to taken to rectify the situation so that an up-to-date, accessible and coherent Statute Book is available to both the organs of government and the citizens who are expected to comply with the law.

If the Statute Book of a country is not currently in an accessible and coherent form, it is necessary to institute a systematic programme of consolidation.[77] If the existing Statute Book consists of legislation that is a hotchpotch of principal Acts, stand-alone amending Acts and non-textual amendments, it will be necessary to recruit a team of people experienced in drafting and editing legislation to systematically prepare consolidated versions of the existing statutes. As far as possible, this should be undertaken on the basis of one statute per topic. For example, there should be one statute dealing with companies; one statute dealing with road traffic; one statute dealing with animal welfare; one statute dealing with criminal law; and so on.

---

[76] Eg like the reprinted laws of Hong Kong.

[77] I use the term 'consolidation' in the way used by Sir Courtenay Ilbert (n 17).

A single authority should be designated to oversee the programme of consolidation. Its function should be to set targets and priorities and to check the appropriateness of draft consolidations. It should be empowered to ordain that particular legislation should be included in the programme, irrespective of the wishes of government departments, some of which are notoriously reluctant to promote consolidations of legislation for which they have administrative responsibility. In most Australian jurisdictions, the relevant Parliamentary Counsel Office has assumed or been accorded responsibility for this kind of function and this has proved successful. Because few people are likely to understand legislation better than those who write it, arguably parliamentary counsel are the people best placed to fulfil this role.

As is the case with revisions in Canadian jurisdictions and reprints in most Australian jurisdictions, the consolidation team should be authorised to make changes such as:

- removing obvious inconsistencies between different provisions;
- standardising the wording of frequently used provisions;
- shortening long sections and subsections by splitting them into shorter and more readable provisions;
- ensuring the consistent use of gender-neutral language; and
- eradicating archaic expressions (including Latinisms).

In conjunction with the consolidation programme, a firm decision needs to be taken to ensure that all future amendments to statutes and statutory rules are made only by the textual method. This should even extend to savings and transitional provisions contained in amending legislation. In the rare occasions where non-textual global referential amendments are required, they should be converted to textual amendments at the earliest opportunity.

Once the consolidation programme is completed, the Statute Book will then be in a form that will allow statutes and statutory rules to be made available to the public in an updated, accessible and coherent form immediately after they are amended. I envisage that special legislation authorising a designated authority to publish updated statutes and statutory rules as and when appropriate. This legislation could be on the lines of Part 6A of the *Interpretation Act 1987* (NSW), but it could equally be on the lines of Canadian legislation authorising the revision of statutes.[78] Although the preparation of reprinted statutes and statutory rules would become a largely mechanical exercise that could be undertaken by competent clerical staff, I maintain that the most competent people for overseeing the reprints programme would be the local Parliamentary Counsel Office. This is because no one knows their way around statutes and statutory rules better than those who are responsible for drafting them. If the reprint method is adopted, both paper and electronic versions should be produced. To facilitate speedy updating, the paper version should be prepared and maintained in loose-leaf form. Both paper and electronic versions should include:

[78]Eg the *Statute Revision Act* [Revised Statutes of British Columbia 1996] Chapter 440.

- historical notes containing a table of amending statutes or statutory rules; and
- a list showing the provisions that were amended and the dates on which the amendments took effect.

Last but not least, a reprints or revision programme along the lines suggested has to be properly funded if it is to be successfully implemented. Unfortunately, there are few votes in undertaking a reform of the Statute Book. This is compounded by the difficulty in getting consolidation legislation through the legislature, even when there are special rules to ease its way over the legislative hurdles.

Nevertheless, the benefits of having an up-to-date, accessible and coherent Statute Book must surely be obvious. Apart from the removal of the frustration, the cost savings to both the state and the private citizen in both time and effort are surely immense. Moreover, no longer will the government official, lawyer or ordinary citizen have to hunt for the law scattered among umpteen different statutes and statutory rules that are often inconsistent with one another. The money will surely be money well spent!

Acknowledgements

The views expressed in this article are entirely the author's own, but he would like to acknowledge the contributions made by Peter Quiggin, Don Colagiuri, Gemma Varley, Geoff Hackett-Jones, Greg Calcutt, Mike McCluskie and Dawn Ray (all Australia); George Tanner (New Zealand); John Mark Keyes and Janet Erasmus (Canada); Daniel Greenberg (UK); Clive Borrowman (Jersey, Channel Islands); and Kieran Mooney (Ireland).

Notes on contributor

Duncan Berry is a consultant Parliamentary Counsel at the Irish Office of the Parliamentary Counsel to the Government. He holds an LLM, MPP, GDSM, and SJD. He is also the Secretary of the Commonwealth Association of Legislative Counsel and the editor of the Association's Journal 'TheLoophole'.

Drafting by more than words: the use of graphics, labels and formulae in legislation

St John Bates

Visiting Professor, University of Strathclyde Law School and Director, St John Bates Consultancy

To achieve accuracy and also clarity the drafter may, where appropriate, resort, for instance, to graphics, alphabetical labels or algebraic formulae to achieve the necessary accuracy and clarity. This is by no means a new legislative technique but in many jurisdictions there appears to be an increasing contemporary use of it. The article argues that there is no doubt that legislating in other than words, in appropriate circumstances, may contribute to legislative clarity. However, the drafter should be circumspect in assuming that the technique creates greater precision.

Introduction

Those who draft and use legislation are very conscious, even without recourse to the philosophy of language, that words inherently lack precision. To achieve accuracy and also clarity the drafter commonly compensates for this by definitions. However, definitions are also expressed in words and they too may lack precision. So the drafter may resort, for instance, to graphics, alphabetical labels or algebraic formulae to achieve the necessary accuracy and clarity. This is by no means a new legislative technique but in many jurisdictions there appears to be an increasing contemporary use of it. This article reflects on this trend of legislating other than simply by words, drawing predominantly on examples from United Kingdom primary legislation.

Graphics

Illustrations are used here as the example, but structure charts (to present an organisational structure) and algorithms (to guide the user through the operation of provisions as they apply to individual cases, by answering sequential questions) may also, for instance, be used to good effect.

Illustrations, both historically and in contemporary practice, are often used in legislation. A common use is in legislation on traffic signs and road markings. The Traffic Signs Regulations and General Directions 1994,[1] for instance, contain many diagrams and representations of the signs in its Schedules. This is obviously an effective way of presenting the law more clearly than description relying simply on words.

---

[1] S 1 1994/1519.

This may be demonstrated by the statutory description[2] in words, without illustration, of the flag of Samoa:

> Red, the first quarter blue and bearing thereon 5 white regular five-rayed stars representing the Southern Cross the size and disposition of the stars being as follows:
>
> (1) In this prescription the hoist of the flag from top to bottom is regarded as 144 vertical units, and its breadth from side to side as 288 horizontal units.
> (2) Each star has its uppermost point on a vertical line through its centres.
> (3) Two of the stars are disposed with their centres on a vertical line bisecting the blue quarter. The top point of the upper star and bottom points of the lower star are distant 3 vertical units from the upper and lower edges of the blue quarter respectively.
> (4) The star nearest the staff has its top point distant 21 vertical units from the upper edge of the flag, and its nearest point distant 42 horizontal units from the edge nearest
> (5) The star nearest the fly has its top point distant 18 vertical units from the upper edge of the flag, and its nearest point distant 42 horizontal units from the fly edge of the blue quarter.
> (6) The fifth star has its bottom points distant 26 vertical units from the lower edge of the blue quarter and its nearest point distant 56 horizontal units from the fly edge of the blue quarter.
> (7) The star nearest the fly edge measures 15, the topmost star and the star nearest the staff 16, the lowest star 20, and the fifth star 10 vertical units measured from the point of any ray to the point of the next ray but one."

This statutory description, however, also demonstrates the limitation of the statutory illustration. Words may still have to be used to describe matters such as size, including, in appropriate cases, size of lettering, and colour (although that is only generally described in the Samoan example).

Nevertheless, words coupled with an illustration are often an effective legislative technique. UK legislation enacted to protect the symbol of the Olympics defined it as 'the symbol of the International Olympic Committee, consisting of five interlocking rings',[3] but without an illustration. It might be argued that this definition, substantially less elaborate than the Samoan legislative description of the national flag, would have benefited by an illustration of the distinctive manner in which five rings interlock in the symbol – three rings above two, all interlocking, rather than say interlocking linearally.[4]

Alphabetical labels

Abbreviated identification of statutes, bodies and procedures

As a consequence of greater interaction between pieces of legislation, it has become increasingly common to define legislation not simply by reference to the year in the short title, '"the 1980 Act" means the Highways Act 1980',[5] or by a shortened version of the title, 'the "Listed Buildings Act" means the Planning

---

[2]Official Flag and National Anthem of Samoa Act 1994, Schedule.
[3]Olympic Symbol etc (Protection) Act 1995, s 18(1).
[4]The definition might also have benefited by stating the colour of the rings: blue, yellow, black, green and red.
[5]Transport for London Act 2008, s 2.

(Listed Buildings and Conservation Areas) Act 1990',[6] but also by an abbreviation of the short title and its year, '"ITTOIA 2005" means the Income Tax (Trading and Other Income) Act 2005'.[7] Where the abbreviated short title and year is used extensively, though the effect may be accurate and still possibly clear, it is rather inelegant. The UK Finance Act 2008 has 18 statutes referred to in this manner, together with a general interpretative instruction that 'FA' and 'F(No2)A' followed by a year refer, respectively, to the Finance Act and the Finance (No2) Act of that year.[8]

Abbreviations are also now commonly used to identify bodies ('"OFCOM" means the Office of Communications as established by the Office of Communications Act 2002'),[9] procedures ('"NTO case" means a case where a penalty charge has been issued or served under'[10]) and instruments ('the Secretary of State may by order (a "PCT order")' establish or abolish a Primary Care Trust, or vary the area for which it is established).[11] Again, such abbreviations have their advantages and disadvantages.

Alphabetical labelling of persons affected by a provision and of operative conditions of a provision

Traditionally a person affected by a provision is commonly identified by a definition within the chapter or provision. So: 'In this Chapter, "sixth form education" means secondary education suitable to the requirements of pupils who are over compulsory school age'[12] or 'This section applies where a penalty notice has been given to a person ("the employer") under section 22 by a local education authority.'[13]

More recently, there has been something of a renaissance in identifying the person affected by alphabetical label.[14]

Sometimes alphabetical labelling is used to shorten the text and thus clarify it. So:

> (1) This section applies where an application is made to a magistrates' court under section 100 in respect of a person ('P').
> (2) After hearing –

---

[6]Planning Act 2008, s 234.
[7]Finance Act 2008, s 165(1).
[8]Finance Act 2008, s 165.
[9]The 5875-5905 MHz Frequency Band (Management) Regulations 2009 (SI 2009/11), Reg 2.
[10]London Local Authorities and Transport for London Act 2008, s 14(1).
[11]National Health Service Act 2006, s 18(2).
[12]School Standards and Framework Act 1998, s 98A.
[13]Education Skills Act 2008, s 23(1).
[14]It is a technique with a long history. Labelling the individual in the style 'I, AB...' is centuries old in statutory forms and declarations and is still extant (eg Trusts (Scotland) Act 1921, Schedule (form) and the Marriage Act 1949, s 44 (declaration). And the Consumer Credit Act 1974 is famously replete with alphabetically labelling in its scheduled 'examples of use of new terminology' (Sched 2, Pt II (and see s 188)). The usual modern practice is to put the alphabetical label in quotation marks at the point of labelling, but omit them in its subsequent use, but the practice is not always consistent (see the Transport Act 2000, Sched 10, para 17(8)(a)).

(a) the applicant, and
(b) P, if P wishes to be heard, the court may make a violent offender order in respect of P if it is satisfied that the conditions in subsection (3) are met.

(3) The conditions are –
(a) that P is a qualifying offender, and
(b) that P has, since the appropriate date, acted in such a way as to make it necessary to make a violent offender order for the purpose of protecting the public from the risk of serious violent harm caused by P.

(4) When deciding whether it is necessary to make such an order for that purpose, the court must have regard to whether P would, at any time when such an order would be in force, be subject under any other enactment to any measures that would operate to protect the public from the risk of such harm.

(5) A violent offender order may not be made so as to come into force at any time when P –
(a) is subject to a custodial sentence imposed in respect of any offence,
(b) is on licence for part of the term of such a sentence, or
(c) is subject to a hospital order or a supervision order made in respect of any offence.[15]

It can also be conveniently used in conjunction with both separately defined words or phrases and also integrated definitions. So:

(1) This section applies where –
(a) on or after 2nd December 2004, a person ('P') enters into a deferred income agreement in respect of a film in the course of carrying on a trade, and
(b) before P entered into the agreement, event A or event B occurred in relation to the trade in respect of expenditure relating to the film ('the relevant expenditure').

(2) Event A occurs in relation to a trade in respect of expenditure relating to a film when a deduction is made under any of sections 138 to 140 in respect of that expenditure in calculating the profits of the trade of a relevant period ('the deduction').

(3) Event B occurs in relation to a trade in respect of expenditure relating to a film when a claim is made under section 42 of F (No 2) A 1992, in relation to the trade, for a deduction for a relevant period in respect of that expenditure ('the claim') ....

(6) The '15 year period' means the period of 15 years which begins with the operative date.

(7) The 'operative date' means –
(a) where the relevant expenditure is acquisition expenditure only, the date of the acquisition in question, and
(b) in any other case, the date upon which the film is completed.

(8) 'Deferred income agreement in respect of a film' has the same meaning as it has for the purposes of section 142A.

(9) 'Relevant film expenditure' means production or acquisition expenditure relating to the original master version of the film.[16]

However, it is a matter of judgement whether its use is an over-elaborate means of achieving this objective. For example, it is arguable whether using the label 'C' rather than simply referring to 'the child' in the following provision is really worthwhile:

---

[15] Criminal Justice and Immigration Act 2008, s 101.

[16] Income Tax (Trading and Other Income) Act 2005, s 142C; and for another example see s 564.

(1) Where a local authority are providing accommodation for a child ('C') other than by arrangements under section 22C (6)(d), they must not make such arrangements for C unless they have decided to do so in consequence of a review of C's case carried out in accordance with regulations made under section 26.
(2) But subsection (1) does not prevent a local authority making arrangements for C under section 22C(6)(d) if they are satisfied that in order to safeguard C's welfare it is necessary –
    (a) to make such arrangements; and
    (b) to do so as a matter of urgency.[17]

The technique is particularly useful where there are a number of classes of person affected in different ways by the same provision. For instance:

(1) Fingerprints may be taken by an authorised person from a person to whom this section applies.
(2) Fingerprints may be taken under this section only during the relevant period ...
(7) This section applies to –
    (a) any person ('A') who, on being required to do so by an immigration officer on his arrival in the United Kingdom, fails to produce a valid passport with photograph or some other document satisfactorily establishing his identity and nationality or citizenship;
    (b) any person ('B') who has been refused leave to enter the United Kingdom but has been temporarily admitted under paragraph 21 of Schedule 2 to the 1971 Act if an immigration officer reasonably suspects that B might break any condition imposed on him relating to residence or as to reporting to the police or an immigration officer;
    (c) any person ('C') in respect of whom a relevant immigration decision has been made;
    (d) any person ('D') who has been detained under paragraph 16 of Schedule 2 to the 1971 Act or arrested under paragraph 17 of that Schedule;
    (e) any person ('E') who has made a claim for asylum;
    (f) any person ('F') who is a dependant of any of those persons.
(8) 'The relevant period' begins –
    (a) for A, on his failure to produce the passport or other document;
    (b) for B, on the decision to admit him temporarily;
    (c) for C, on the service on him of notice of the relevant immigration decision by virtue of section 105 of the Nationality, Immigration and Asylum Act 2002 (c. 41);
    (d) for D, on his detention or arrest;
    (e) for E, on the making of his claim for asylum; and
    (f) for F, at the same time as for the person whose dependant he is.
(9) 'The relevant period' ends on the earliest of the following –
    (a) the grant of leave to enter or remain in the United Kingdom;
    (b) for A, B, C or D, his removal or deportation from the United Kingdom;
    (c) for C –
        (i) the time when the relevant immigration decision ceases to have effect, whether as a result of an appeal or otherwise, or
        (ii) if a deportation order has been made against him, its revocation or its otherwise ceasing to have effect;
    (d) for D, his release if he is no longer liable to the detained under paragraph 16 of Schedule 2 to the 1971 Act;
    (e) for E, the final determination or abandonment of his claim for asylum; and
    (f) for F, at the same time as for the person whose dependant he is.

---

[17] Children Act 1989, s 22D; the label may have been used because 'child' was similarly labelled in adjacent provisions inserted into the Act.

(10) No fingerprints may be taken from A if the immigration officer considers that A has a reasonable excuse for the failure concerned.
(11) No fingerprints may be taken from B unless the decision to take them has been confirmed by a chief immigration officer.[18]

Although it is a useful device in appropriate cases, this type of alphabetical labelling does raise its own issues.

Sometimes it is used in error. The Criminal Justice and Immigration Act 2008, s 76(1) provides:

> This section applies where in proceedings for an offence –
> (a) an issue arises as to whether a person charged with the offence ('D') is entitled to rely on a defence within subsection (2), and
> (b) the question arises whether the degree of force used by D against a person ('V') was reasonable in the circumstances.

However, while the 'D' label is used several times within the provision, 'V' is not used at all.

Sometimes its use discloses an apparent ambiguity, which one might have thought would have been more easily identified as a result of its use. The Planning Act 2008, s 8 provides:

> (1) In deciding what steps are appropriate for the purposes of section 7(5), the Secretary of State must consult –
> (a) each local authority that is within subsection (2) or (3), and
> (b) the Greater London Authority, if any of the locations concerned is in Greater London.
> (2) A local authority is within this subsection if any of the locations concerned is in the authority's area.
> (3) A local authority ('A') is within this subsection if –
> (a) any of the locations concerned is in the area of another local authority ('B'), and
> (b) any part of the boundary of A's area is also a part of the boundary of B's area.

It is not immediately clear from s 8(3)(b) whether consultation of local authority A is required where a location is in the area of local authority B and any of the areas of the two local authorities overlap, or only required where the location is actually within the overlapping areas of the two local authorities.

Then there are some drafting considerations in the use of the alphabetical label. First, placing the label as close as possible to what is labelled usually enhances clarity. So, 'The gametes of a person ("C") may be kept in storage without C's consent if the following conditions are met'[19] is preferable to 'For the purposes of section 133A(5) this section applies to any case where the person concerned ("P") has been in qualifying detention for a period … of at least ten years by the time when…',[20] and certainly to 'The appropriate body may not approve a research project for the purposes of this Act unless satisfied that the following requirements will be met in

[18] Immigration and Asylum Act 1999, s 141.
[19] Human Fertilisation and Embryology Act 1990, Sched 3, para 9(1).
[20] Criminal Justice Act 1988, s 133B(1).

relation to research carried out as part of the project on, or in relation to, a person who lacks capacity to consent to taking part in the project ("P").'[21]

Secondly, it is desirable to indicate to which provisions the label is applicable. 'Sections 35 to 47 apply, in the case of a child who is being, or has been, carried by a woman (referred to in those sections as "W").'[22] is better drafting practice than allowing it to be assumed that the label also applies to a subsequent provision.[23]

Finally, multiple use of the same label in one statute has at least the potential for confusion. So in the Mental Capacity Act 2005, 'R' is used as a label for a person who '(a) conducting an approved research project, and (b) wishes to carry out research, as part of the project, on or in relations to a person (P) who lack capacity to consent to taking part in the project'[24] and elsewhere for 'a receiver … for a person (P) appointed under section 99 of the Mental Health Act'.[25] More intensively, in the Income Tax (Trading and Other Income) Act 2005, 'P' is variously used as a label for, 'the tax year of which those profits are higher';[26] 'the premium';[27] 'the lesser of – (a) the profit on the assignment, and (b) the amount by which the undervalue exceeds the total of the profits (if any) made on previous assignments of the lease, and Y is the number of complete periods of 12 months (other than the first) comprised in the effective duration of the lease';[28] 'a person other than the recipient';[29] 'a person who is not connected with the issuer';[30] 'any other party to the future or option';[31] 'a person with such an absolute interest'[32] and 'the individual's Part 3 rent-a-room receipts for the tax year'.[33]

Alphabetical and numerical labelling of operative conditions of a provision

Operative conditions of a provision may similarly be alphabetically labelled. Again this may be an appropriate technique where there are various applications. So:

> (3) … In Case A or Case B below, this subsection has effect subject to, and in accordance with, subsection (3C) below.
>
> (3A) Case A is where the offender was aged 18 or over when he committed the offence and the court is of the opinion that the seriousness of the offence, or of the combination of the offence and one or more other offences associated with it, –

[21] Mental Capacity Act 2005, s 31(1); an additional reason for changing the position of the label here is that on a first reading it might be unclear whether the label is attached to 'person' or 'project'.
[22] Human Fertilisation and Embryology Act 2008, s 34.
[23] Eg Income Tax (Earnings and Pensions) Act 2003, ss 100A, 100B; although in that case it could be readily assumed from the context.
[24] S 32(1).
[25] Sched 5 para 1(1).
[26] S 223(4)(b).
[27] S 277(4).
[28] S 282(4).
[29] S 397(5).
[30] S 431(6).
[31] S 564(6).
[32] S 673(2).
[33] S 797(5).

(a) is exceptional (but not such that the court proposes to make an order under subsection (4) below), and
(b) would not be adequately reflected by the period which the court would otherwise specify under subsection (2) above.

(3B) Case B is where the court is of the opinion that the period which it would otherwise specify under subsection (2) above would have little or no effect on time spent in custody, taking into account all the circumstances of the particular offender.

(3C) In Case A or Case B above, in deciding the effect which the comparison required by subsection (3) (c) above is to have on reducing the period which the court determines for the purposes of subsection (3)(a) (and before giving effect to subsection (3)(b) above), the court may, instead of reducing that period by one-half, –
(a) in Case A above, reduce it by such lesser amount (including nil) as the court may consider appropriate according to the seriousness of the offence, or
(b) in Case B above, reduce it by such lesser amount (but not by less than one-third) as the court may consider appropriate in the circumstances.[34]

However, it is also again a matter of judgement whether applying the technique is appropriate. In the following example, it is arguable that an equally clear and accurate presentation would have been achieved by substituting the labelled conditions with 'and the terms of subsections (2)–(4) are satisfied':

(1) This section applies where there are two companies which are connected and conditions A, B and C are met.
(2) Condition A is…
(3) Condition B is…
(4) Condition C is…[35]

Sometimes operative provisions may be numbered. So, for instance, the Income Tax Act 2007 presents calculation procedures as a series of numbered 'steps'.[36] This provides clarity, but it might also perhaps be presented diagrammatically with equal clarity.

Algebraic formulae

There is a long tradition in financial legislation of using algebraic formulae to describe the operation of a provision, but the technique may be used in other legislation. So, for instance, the Planning Act 2008, s 24 (4)–(6) provides:

(4) For the purposes of subsection (3)(d), facilities are capable of handling an equivalent quantity of material if the sum of the relevant fractions is one or more.
(5) The relevant fractions are –
(a) to the extent that the facilities are for container ships –
x/500,000
where x is the number of TEU that the facilities are capable of handling;
(b) to the extent that the facilities are for ro-ro ships –

[34] Powers of the Criminal Courts (Sentencing) Act 2000, s 82A; for examples of similar numerical labelling see Criminal Justice and Immigration Act 2008, ss 130.
[35] Finance Act 1996, s 94B (repealed by the Corporation Tax Act 2009).
[36] Eg ss 809J, 809Q.

y/250,000
where y is the number of units that the facilities are capable of handling;

(c) to the extent that the facilities are for cargo ships of any other description –
z/5,000,000
where z is the number of tonnes of material that the facilities are capable of handling.

(6) In this section –
'cargo ship' means a ship which is used for carrying cargo;
'container ship' means a cargo ship which carries all or most of its cargo in containers;
'ro-ro ship' means a ship which is used for carrying wheeled cargo;
'TEU' means a twenty-foot equivalent unit;
'unit' in relation to a ro-ro ship means any item of wheeled cargo (whether or not self-propelled).[37]

In financial legislation the algebraic formulae is often more complex. So:

For the purposes of section 1113 the total R&D aid, in respect of expenditure by a company ('the claimant') attributable to a research and development project, is calculated as follows –
$A = (TC + R + (P \times CT)) - (N \times CT)$

Where –

A is the total R&D aid,
TC is the tax credits (see section 1115),
R is the actual reduction in tax liability (see section 1116),
P is the potential relief (see section 1117),
CT is the main rate of corporation tax at the time when the total R&D aid is calculated, and
N is the notional relief (see section 1118).[38]

And as can be seen from that illustration, the more complex the formula, the greater the likelihood that more textual provision is needed to explain its operation.

As with alphabetical labelling, the drafter may need to ask whether the use of algebraic formula is really needed to express the law accurately and clearly. The matter is perhaps finely balanced in this final example.

If the whole of a transitional chargeable period falls within a financial year listed in column 1 of the table (for corporation tax purposes) or a tax year listed in column 2 of the table (for income tax purposes), the writing-down allowance to which the person is entitled for that chargeable period is–
$WDA \times P$

Where –

WDA is the writing-down allowance to which the person would be entitled for the chargeable period apart from this section, and
P is the percentage specified in relation to that year in column 3 of the table.[39]

---

[37] For another area where it has been used see the Housing Act 1985, s 143B.
[38] Competition Act 2009, s 1114.
[39] Finance Act 2008, s 85(3).

Conclusion

There is no doubt that legislating in other than words, in appropriate circumstances, may contribute to legislative clarity. However, the drafter should be circumspect in assuming that the technique creates greater precision. If only because it can rarely be deployed without the use of words. And as Lord Diplock once observed, echoing Humpty Dumpty, 'Words mean whatever they are said to mean by a majority of the members of the [House of Lords] dealing with the case, even though a minority may think otherwise.'[40]

Notes on contributor

St John Bates is the Director of the St John Bates Consultancy (a subsidiary of Bates Enterprises Ltd) which offers legislative drafting services internationally (www.stjohn batesconsultancy.com), a Visiting Professor at the University of Strathclyde Law School in Scotland and an Associate Senior Research Fellow, Institute of Advanced Legal Studies, University of London.

---

[40] *Carter v Bradbeer* [1975] 1 WLR 1204, 1205 (HL).

The challenges of legislative drafting in small Commonwealth jurisdictions

Ranjit Hewagama

Consultant, Omar Associates Attorneys-at-Law, Colombo, Sri Lanka

It is widely accepted that many legal challenges facing small Commonwealth jurisdictions today are common to all countries, both large and small. However, it is equally true that many of these challenges are more acute and prevail to a large extent in smaller jurisdictions. Legislative drafting is one such challenge. The shortage of legislative drafting expertise impedes implementation of policies and government legislative programmes. It is quite apparent that the problems faced in small jurisdictions appear to be more acute than those of larger Commonwealth countries. This reflects the necessity for small Commonwealth states to adopt, apart from the solutions advocated to meet common challenges, special procedures, policies and infrastructure at a national level.

Introduction

Having worked in three Commonwealth states, namely, Sri Lanka, Jamaica and the Solomon Islands in the Pacific, over a period of 35 years, I will endeavour to state briefly my experiences as a legal drafter and the challenges encountered whilst working in small Commonwealth jurisdictions.

It is widely accepted that many legal challenges facing small Commonwealth jurisdictions today are common to all countries, both large and small. However, it is equally true that many of these challenges are more acute and prevail to a large extent in smaller jurisdictions. Legislative drafting being one such challenge.

The attainment of independence by small states in the Caribbean and Pacific brought about increased legal activity in these states. These countries needed to enact legislation in keeping with the constitutional provisions that granted their independence. The range of legislation that had to be provided was as wide and diverse as that of a large Commonwealth state.

Constitutions of independent Commonwealth states

One of the most important aspect of government in any jurisdiction is the capacity to make its own laws. All former colonies, protectorates and dependencies, which were governed by the British, were granted independence by Independence Orders.

These Independence Orders established new sovereign democratic states and their constitutions. One of the main characteristics of these written constitutions was the inclusion of a chapter on 'Fundamental Rights and Freedoms of the Individual'. The purpose of incorporating fundamental rights in a written constitution is to ensure that certain principles cannot be altered or taken away by the ordinary process of legislation. Where there is a written constitution, it is the supreme law of the country. Justice Sharvananda, a former Chief Justice of Sri Lanka, in his book titled *Fundamental Rights in Sri Lanka* states 'the Constitution is a basic norm. The Constitution generates its own validity. The Constitution is binding because it is the Constitution. Any other law is binding only if and so far as it is in conformity with the Constitution.'[1]

This is because a written constitution lays down certain limitations and all other laws enacted must be within the ambit of that constitution. Great care is needed to ensure that nothing is drafted which would be inconsistent with, or in contravention of, the provisions of the constitution of a country.

Sources of legislation

The primary source of legislation in Commonwealth countries is an Act of Parliament. An Act of Parliament is presented to Parliament in the form of a 'Bill'. When it is passed by Parliament it transforms itself into an 'Act of Parliament'. The Act so enacted lays down the principles governing a particular subject matter.

Process of legislation

All Bills originate from a policy document. This is the normal and accepted procedure. The policy document or proposal goes through a long process before it reaches Parliament in the form of a Bill. It is during this process that a drafter in a small Commonwealth jurisdiction is confronted with many challenges. A policy document or proposal is generally initiated by the particular ministry of the Government to which the subject matter is assigned. The proposal is first submitted by the particular ministry to Cabinet for approval, to be adopted as Government policy. The Cabinet submission further seeks approval for the issuing of drafting instructions to the drafter of the Bill. On receipt of Cabinet approval, the ministry is required to issue detailed drafting instructions. These instructions should, in detail, outline the reasons and the background of the proposals, the present state of the law on the particular issue, or the absence of such law to deal with the particular situation and the measures outlined in the proposal to remedy the defect.

Role of the drafter

A drafter's role in formulating a draft Bill based on the available instructions, whatever the jurisdiction, is always painstaking and challenging. The challenges and problems in one country may not be uncommon to other jurisdictions but may be more profound in smaller Commonwealth jurisdictions.

The functions of a drafter are to draft legislation in clear and unambiguous language so as to give effect to the intentions of the legislature. Where there is

---

[1] S Sharvananda, *Fundamental Rights in Sri Lanka* (Colombo, Sri Lanka 1993).

ambiguity in the Act or where the Statute does not in clear words express the intention of the legislature, questions of interpretation arise. A drafter's responsibility will, therefore, be to use words in a Statute that are clear and seek to achieve accuracy and precision. The challenges that a drafter encounters in producing the final Bill through this long process to a great extent depends on the particular jurisdiction.

Challenges in small Commonwealth jurisdictions

In order to implement Government policies and legislative programmes, there is need either to introduce new legislation or amend existing legislation. The shortage of legislative drafting expertise impedes implementation of policies and legislative programmes of the governments of these countries. Some of the challenges faced by Pacific small island jurisdictions, such as the Solomon Islands, are evident when a comparative analysis is done with that of a fairly larger Commonwealth jurisdiction, such as Sri Lanka or Jamaica.

Structure of ministries and drafting instructions

In Sri Lanka or Jamaica, a drafter's task is that much less burdensome than in a small Commonwealth jurisdiction. In such countries, a drafter is generally provided with reasonably good quality drafting instructions. During my time as a drafter in Sri Lanka in the early 1970s, a Legal Research Division existed at the Ministry of Justice. In Jamaica, a Law Reform Division was in existence in the Ministry of Legal Affairs during my tenure as a Parliamentary Draftsman.

The structure of the Ministry of Justice (Legal Affairs) to a great extent facilitates the issuance of good drafting instructions. Where a subject has been studied deeply and argued fully as a result of discussions, clear and precise drafting instructions are issued. This is of immense assistance to a drafter. Such is generally the case where instructions are issued based on recommendations made on a study done by a law research or law reform unit.

In the Solomon Islands at present, the Law Reform Commission has been reactivated and is engaged in meaningful law reform activities. However, the Commission does not play any role in the drafting process, unless it is a Bill that originates from a proposal or recommendation made by it. Another major drawback in some Pacific small island jurisdictions is that the Legal Draftsman's Division is a part of the Attorney General's Chambers and drafters are, at times, called upon to handle litigation and other legal matters apart from drafting. The establishment of a Drafting Division as a separate department will ensure, to an extent, the provision of a more effective drafting service.

Another factor that contributes to the non-issuance of adequate drafting instructions in a Pacific small island jurisdiction, like the Solomon Islands, is the non-existence of legal officers in government ministries. In Sri Lanka and Jamaica, almost all ministries are staffed with in-house legal advisers. This enables a drafter to consult and seek clarification on any intricate or technical issues that may arise in the drafting process. In most Pacific small island jurisdictions none of the ministries are staffed by in-house legal officers. In most instances, there are very few ministry officers who could provide proper guidance on matters affecting the substance of a Bill. The reason for this being that such officials, to a great extent, rely on expatriate consultants for assistance. These consultants, at most times, prepare draft legislation and leave the country without adequately briefing their local counterparts on such draft legislation. In some instances, it has been discovered that these consultants have advocated small Commonwealth jurisdictions to follow legal developments in larger jurisdictions, even to the extent of adopting legislation that is inappropriate to such small Commonwealth jurisdictions. It should be highlighted that consultants should be required to adequately brief their local counterparts and work in tandem with the local drafter.

In Pacific small island jurisdictions, a drafter is very often involved in advising a government on policy matters. This in itself is not a bad practice, as a drafter could at an early stage adequately advise the Government of the legal implications of a proposal.

Legal resources

A legal resource that is lacking in small Commonwealth jurisdictions is legal literature. This means the existence of an updated set of revised laws, legal texts, law reports and a good law library. However, it appears that modern technology helps to overcome this problem. Legal drafters now have access to PacLii, Lexis and other legal data bases. In the Solomon Islands, there existed a good collection of laws and statutes (including editions of H*alsbury's Laws and Statutes*), Acts of the United Kingdom, Proclamations and Orders in Council, etc. However, it is regrettable that most lawyers and drafters do not appreciate the value of these resources. Furthermore, with the advent of modern technology, these valuable resources have unfortunately been relegated to storage. It should be highlighted that, in my view, these resources are invaluable when it comes to researching the origins of a legal concept and legal precedents.

In the Solomon Islands, the last Revised Edition of the *Laws* was published in 1995. The previous edition had been published in 1969. The publication of the Annual Volumes of Legislation had ceased in 1982. The state of the law was uncertain. In addition, the Government Gazettes were not published on a regular basis. Practitioners, therefore, relied to a great extent on the Attorney General's Chambers to apprise them whether an Act or subsidiary legislation was in force. Access to an updated version of current legislation is of essence in providing quality legislation.

In the Solomon Islands, in terms of the Constitution, a law which originates in the form of a Bill, when passed by Parliament, has to be presented to the Governor General for assent. Once the Bill is assented to, it becomes law. No law comes into operation until it is published in the Gazette. The drafter's task, which commences in most instances from the time of the first proposal being submitted to the Cabinet, does not end with the passage of the Bill by Parliament. Due to the scarcity of junior drafters and support staff, the drafter is required to personally supervise and follow through the entire process of finalisation of the Bill with the Government Printer, which includes proof-reading, visiting the printers, supervising the typesetting, formatting, etc. As such, in Pacific small island jurisdictions, like the Solomon Islands, Governments need to understand the importance of providing the requisite support staff to the drafting offices.

Publication

The Interpretation and General Provisions Act of the Solomon Islands requires that subsidiary legislation made under an Act be placed before Parliament. All subsidiary legislation in terms of the Act needs to be published in the Gazette as Legal Notices. In the Solomon Islands this requirement was not strictly complied with. Due to this state of affairs, the Government in 2005 enacted a Bill entitled *Interpretation and General Provisions (Validation and Indemnity) Act 2005*, validating all acts done in good faith by officials in the exercise of certain functions and powers conferred on them by subsidiary legislation passed between the years 1996 and 2005. There is, therefore, an urgent need for the Government to pay more attention to the strengthening of the capacity of the Government Printing Office and also to the training of public officers on legislative procedures.

Shortage of drafters

It is well accepted that in most countries there is a shortage of drafters, especially in small developing Commonwealth jurisdictions. The Solomon Islands is no exception to this. When I assumed office as Legal Draftsman in 1985, there was only one assistant drafter in the Attorney General's Chambers. During the period 1985 to 2007, several juniors at various intervals joined the drafting division but kept moving out to either join the private bar or taking on other jobs in the private sector, regional or international funded organisations. One of the main reasons for drafters moving out was the unsatisfactory working conditions and poor pay. Though various attempts were made to remedy this situation, there was little success. A probable solution to this situation may lie in the introduction of a separate and distinct cadre for drafters from the rest of the public service, with an attractive and exclusive pay structure for them.

In Pacific small island jurisdictions, due to the shortage of drafters, it is not possible to successfully implement a proper in-house training programme. In larger jurisdictions, such as Sri Lanka or Jamaica, a junior drafter or pupil is assigned to a senior drafter. This enables drafters to operate in pairs; thus enabling the juniors to be under the supervision and guidance of a more experienced drafter. This system worked well in both Sri Lanka and Jamaica. The Chief Parliamentary Counsel or Legal Draftsman, in fact, enters the arena only at the stage when the Bill has gone through a number of drafts and contentious issues thoroughly discussed and sorted out. In small Commonwealth jurisdictions, due to the shortage of drafters, this important element of 'pairing' and 'mentoring' does not operate satisfactorily.

Legislative programme

In most larger Commonwealth jurisdictions, there is in place a legislative programme. This programme is generally prepared by the Cabinet Office, with input from ministries. Each ministry, at the conclusion of the year, submits to Cabinet its proposed legislation for the ensuing year. The Cabinet Office thereafter prepares a Government legislative programme indicating what it considers 'Priority Bills'. In most instances, governments adhere to the approved programme; the only deviation being 'Finance or Revenue Bills' and Bills considered urgent on the basis of public policy. This practice does not prevail in the Solomon Islands and probably not in other Pacific small island jurisdictions as well. The Government of the Solomon Islands should seriously consider implementing such a legislative programme in order to facilitate the work of the Drafter.

Comments on drafting

Drafts require constant revision taking into account the feedback received on drafts circulated for examination and comment, which is time-consuming. Constructive comments rarely reach the drafter. This is more so when a piece of legislation is externally sponsored. This does cause concern to the drafter, as in some instances such drafts do not conform to accepted formats or precedents. In most instances, there are deviations from the precedents followed in the particular jurisdiction, as the consultants, in most instances, are unfamiliar with the legal background of the particular country. It is, therefore, important that all drafts prepared by consultants be done in consultation with the local drafter.

Meeting of heads of drafting offices in the Asia region

The above-mentioned meeting was organised by the Commonwealth Secretariat and held in Malaysia in January 2008. I participated at the meeting as a resource person.

The main issue discussed at the meeting was the ways and means of dealing with the shortage of legislative drafters in drafting offices. It was noted that the shortage of legislative drafters was an ongoing problem in drafting offices in the region. It also identified challenges that were common in most of the Asia region, which included the

- lack of properly structured offices;
- lack of recognition of drafters;
- inadequate drafting instructions;
- lack of interest by the relevant authorities; and
- poor terms and conditions of service.

It must be emphasised that these common challenges are not uniform in application, as countries, such as India, Sri Lanka and some larger Commonwealth jurisdictions, are better geared to face them.

Conclusion

The foregoing is an attempt to highlight the challenges associated with drafting in small Commonwealth jurisdictions, especially in Pacific small island states. It is quite apparent that the problems faced in a small jurisdiction, such as the Solomon Islands, appear to be more acute than those of a larger Commonwealth jurisdiction. This reflects the necessity for small Commonwealth states to adopt, apart from the solutions advocated to meet common challenges, special procedures, policies and infrastructure at a national level.

Notes on contributor

Ranjit Hewagama CBE is a legislative drafting consultant and a consultant with Omar Associates Attorneys-at-Law, Colombo, Sri Lanka. He holds an LLB from the University of Ceylon and has extensive experience in the area of legislative drafting having, amongst others, held the following positions: Assistant Legal Draftsman, Sri Lanka, 1972–1975; Assistant Parliamentary Counsel, Jamaica, 1975–1978; Parliamentary Counsel, Jamaica, 1978–1985; Legal Draftsman, the Solomon Islands, 1985–2007 (1998–2001 Legal Draftsman/Solicitor General); Chairman, Law Revision Commission, the Solomon Islands; and Member of the Judicial and Legal Services Commission, the Solomon Islands.

Fact Sheets

Building a commons for the common law: the Commonwealth Legal Information Institute (CommonLII) four years on

Graham Greenleaf, Andrew Mowbray and Philip Chung

Co-directors, AustLII and CommonLII

The Commonwealth Legal Information Institute (CommonLII – http://www.commonlii.org – pronounced 'Common-lee'), is a non-profit and free access website for legal information from all countries that are members of the Commonwealth and their territories (more than 60). CommonLII also covers a small number of significant non-Commonwealth countries and territories that have a legal system based on the common law, including the Republic of Ireland and the Hong Kong Special Administrative Region (SAR).

The main purpose of CommonLII is to provide a comparative law facility by which the laws of all common law countries can be searched and compared. In relation to case law, CommonLII assists in making the ideal of an international common law a reality, by providing the case law collection with the broadest geographical scope, and the only free access international citator (LawCite). In relation to legislation, CommonLII makes it easier to compare legislative developments in the same subject-areas across Commonwealth countries, and can therefore assist in the process of law reform, as well as increasing the transparency of each country's legal system. CommonLII also makes it easier to find commentaries on the law from Commonwealth and common law countries, including law reform reports and some law journals.

Partners, scope and supporters

CommonLII is a cooperative development by existing providers of free access to law facilities (usually called 'legal information institutes' or 'LIIs' for short) in Commonwealth and common law countries. At the end of 2009, CommonLII provided a facility to search 795 databases, of which 726 were maintained by eight other LIIs. These were (in alphabetical order) AustLII (Australia – 375), BAILII (Great Britain and Ireland – 78), CyLaw (Cyprus – 6), HKLII (Hong Kong – 13), NZLII (New Zealand – 35) PacLII (Pacific Island countries and territories including Papua New Guinea – 156), SAFLII (15 countries in Southern and Eastern Africa – 56) and ULII (Uganda – 7). These LIIs from Commonwealth countries are a major part of the global Free Access to Law Movement, whose ideals are set out in the Declaration on Free Access to Law (2002).[1]

---

[1]See Annex I.

The CommonLII web portal is developed and maintained by the Australasian Legal Information Institute (AustLII). Sixty-nine databases from 25 Commonwealth countries and territories with no separate local LII[2] are included on the CommonLII system itself, and maintained by AustLII. The other 37 Commonwealth countries already have their own national or regional LIIs, so their data is included in CommonLII via the networking arrangements between CommonLII and other LIIs.

CommonLII was proposed in 2003 at the Commonwealth Law Conference in Melbourne.[3] In 2005 it was launched at the Commonwealth Law Conference in London, and it was also presented to the Commonwealth Senior Law Officers Meeting in London in 2007.

In October 2005 the Commonwealth Law Ministers, meeting in Ghana, resolved that

> Commonwealth Law Ministers welcomed the development of the Commonwealth Legal Information Institute (CommonLII). The Meeting noted that CommonLII is an Internet research facility providing free access to legal information from all Commonwealth countries. The Meeting encouraged all countries to cooperate in the development of CommonLII by providing, to the extent possible, access to their legal materials, including legislation, case law and law reform reports.

A number of Commonwealth institutions have also expressed their support for CommonLII, including the Legal and Constitutional Affairs Division of the Commonwealth Secretariat (LCAD/COMSEC), the Commonwealth Lawyers Association, the Commonwealth Magistrates' and Judges' Association, the Institute of Advanced Legal Studies (IALS) and the Commonwealth Legal Education Association (CLEA).[4]

Content from each country

For every country on CommonLII, there are included on that country's main page: (i) the searchable databases from that country; (ii) an index of law-related websites from that country (and a means of searching them); and (iii) a means of searching the web for law from that country, using the Google search engine.

Types of databases, and their scope

The searchable databases available on CommonLII for Commonwealth and common law countries are:

---

[2]Antigua & Barbuda; The Bahamas; Bangladesh; Barbados; Belize; Brunei; Dominica; The Gambia; Ghana; Grenada; Guyana; India; Jamaica; Malaysia; Maldives; Malta; Nigeria; Sierra Leone; Singapore; Sri Lanka; St Kitts & Nevis; St Lucia; St Vincent & Grenadines; Trinidad & Tobago; and (most recently) Rwanda. Canada has its own LII, but it has decided not to participate in CommonLII.

[3]G Greenleaf, P Chung and A Mowbray, 'A New Home Online for Commonwealth Law: A Proposal for a CommonLII' (2004) 2 JILT, ⟨http://www2.warwick.ac.uk/fac/soc/law/elj/jilt/2004_2/greenleafmowbrayandchung/⟩.

[4]See 'Commonwealth Supporting Institutions' on the 'Stakeholders' page on CommonLII.

- Over 700,000 Court decisions from almost all countries, usually including the decisions of the highest courts of those countries. Their comprehensiveness varies a great deal. These include the 125,000 decisions comprising the *English Reports (1220–1873)*, which constitute the foundations of the common law and, as such, are CommonLII's 'crown jewels', and not available elsewhere for free access.
- The Constitutions of most countries.
- Legislation from over 40 countries, with comprehensive sets consolidated to include amendments from some jurisdictions (eg Singapore, New Zealand, Australia, the United Kingdom, and Sri Lanka).
- Law reform reports from 20 law reform bodies in 10 countries.
- Over 60 law journals including more than 20,000 articles, mostly from Australia and New Zealand, but with an increasing number from Commonwealth institutions, Pacific Island countries, and the UK.
- Treaties from a few countries, including the comprehensive Australian Treaties Library, and additional treaties from Singapore and from Pacific Island countries.
- Every country has a 'virtual database' which includes content concerning that country drawn from other LIIs and databases, such as treaties or international court decisions to which the country is a party, or journal articles concerning it.
- The LawCite citator ⟨http://www.commonlii.org/LawCite/⟩ is the only free access international case citator available on the Internet. It provides citation histories for almost 3 million cases, the majority of which are from common law countries.

In all of these categories, these are the most extensive searchable databases for this kind of legal information across common law countries.

Extent of coverage

In terms of the comprehensiveness of the databases on CommonLII, countries fall into three broad categories:

- The best scenario is where the Courts or Justice agencies of a country actively provide their decisions, legislation or law reform reports to a local legal information institute like SAFLII, PacLII, BAILII or AustLII. This reduces the resources needed by the LII, improves consistency, and helps keep the information up to date. All of the other LIIs whose content is included in CommonLII receive this form of active assistance. As discussed in the conclusion, AustLII would like to develop such data provision arrangements in other Commonwealth countries wherever it is possible to do so.
- The minimum coverage is that we only include the Constitution(s) from the country, plus a virtual database of other LII content relating to that country. This is all that is included at present from Sierra Leone, The Gambia, the Maldives and Guyana, but for all other countries there are somewhat more substantial collections.

- For 25 countries, the legal information made available on free access official websites is republished on CommonLII, usually first converted into a consistent format for search purposes. The copyright laws of most Commonwealth countries allow such republication, and in other cases it is authorised by licences. This approach provides some key databases from almost all Commonwealth countries, but sometimes of limited scope. In some cases, this 'web republication' approach results in a large number of databases, or some very large databases, being available because of very active government web publication policies. Examples are Sri Lanka, India and Singapore.

Demonstration searches

This section will provide some search examples to demonstrate the features of CommonLII.

Comparative law searches across all countries

An example of a comparative law search across all 558 databases on CommonLII is to research the question of which Commonwealth countries have implemented laws on money laundering. Starting with a simple search on CommonLII's front page for the phrase 'money laundering' returns nearly 2800 results, ranked by relevance. This demonstrates that there is considerable legislation across the Commonwealth on this topic. The first page of results includes legislation from Australia, Belize, Samoa, Cook Islands, Solomon Islands, Malta, Tonga, Nigeria, and the UK – and that's just the first page. We can also use the By Database display option and 'Collapse listing' to see where the results come from – in this instance, they come from 201 databases in 22 countries. If we sort the results By Date we find many recent cases dealing with this issue.

There is no other research facility on either free access or commercial systems that will let you do this type of comparative research across all or even most common law countries, or to find recent materials so easily. Searches such as this demonstrate a key element of CommonLII's approach: by allowing one search over all of the available legislation, case law, law journal articles, and other content, we are able to make more sense of each type of content, and to make research more efficient.

Searching only one country – 'one-stop shopping' research

CommonLII can also be used to search for law from only one country. Choosing India as an example we first go to the India page in the list of Commonwealth countries on CommonLII's front page. Methods of alternative dispute resolution are important, particular to investors and other foreign parties interested in the laws of a particular country. A search for all forms of alternative dispute resolution would be something like the following:[5]

arbitrat* or mediat* or alternative dispute resolution or ADR

---

[5]The asterisk '*' is used to truncate words to their stems.

This search query returns 3700 results ranked in likely order of relevance (a 1984 case is highest ranked, followed by two Acts concerning arbitration). These results may also be sorted By Date to find the most recent results, or By Database to see which of 24 different Indian databases the results came from.

In addition, there are three other methods shown on the India page (and other country pages) by which CommonLII assists in finding legal material from this country anywhere on the Internet (not only in CommonLII's databases).

(i) The *Catalogue* of the country's law websites (at the bottom of the country's page), which is likely to include a category for 'Alternative Dispute Resolution' providing links to other useful websites (eg. Indian Council of Arbitration).
(ii) The previous search terms (used to search the databases) can be re-used to do a '*Websearch*' of many of the sites listed in the Catalogue relating to India. Individual pages containing the search keywords from many of these sites are then found.
(iii) Finally, using the '*Law on Google*' option will send the same search terms to Google's search engine. CommonLII converts the search into the proper search language for Google, and limits the results to legal materials concerning ADR in India.

Searches such as this demonstrate the main aim of the CommonLII country pages: to be, as far as possible, a 'one-stop shop' for extensive legal research concerning that country, using as many different channels and research techniques as possible. Searching CommonLII's databases, plus the three additional methods above, will almost always provide useful results.

Future development of CommonLII

After over four years of gradual development (including major additions such as the 125,000 cases of the *English Reports* and the LawCite citator), in 2010, CommonLII is set to enter a phase of rapid expansion.

Firstly, the other LIIs whose partnerships are the cornerstone of CommonLII are thriving, and providing an ever-increasing number of databases whose content may be searched via CommonLII, and whose cases are citation-tracked by LawCite. In the last two years the number of databases searchable via CommonLII has increased by over 200, with major contributions from SAFLII, PacLII, BAILII, and AustLII. Thirty-seven Commonwealth countries and territories now have their databases kept up to date by their own national or regional free access legal information institutes.

Major new LIIs in Commonwealth countries are now under development. AusAID has provided funding for 2010–11 to AustLII to assist the development of a new Indian LII, in cooperation with four leading Indian law schools, and it is expected that this will be launched in 2010. This project will also expand free access to law in other South Asian Commonwealth countries (Bangladesh, Sri Lanka, Pakistan and the Maldives).

LCAD/COMSEC has provided assistance to promote the free access to law development in the Caribbean, a region which is currently under-represented in the

CommonLII searchable database. In this respect, a Caribbean Law Project on CommonLII ⟨http://www.commonlii.org/caribbean/⟩ has been developed to facilitate this, with a view to the gradual development of a Caribbean LII.[6]

The Australian Research Council has also provided major funding of over A$400,000[7] for 2010–11 to AustLII for a project entitled 'Free Access Legal Research Infrastructure for the Whole of the Common Law: Completing CommonLII', which will enable AustLII to build substantial databases for all Commonwealth countries which do not have their own LIIs, and encourage the development of such LIIs.

The Australian Attorney-General's Department has also continued to provide funding for CommonLII since its inception. Details of all funding for CommonLII are available on AustLII's 'Funding for International Projects' page (http://www.austlii.edu.au/cgi-bin/s_juris.cgi?int).

Once separate national or regional LIIs emerge to maintain the databases from South Asia and the Caribbean, and a number of West African countries have their own LIIs, or are included in SAFLII, CommonLII will come close to being a self-sustaining system. Its role in assisting the creation of an international common law will then be a permanent reality.

As well as expanding the coverage of CommonLII, AustLII is developing new services based on specific subject areas of law. The first of these, developed with funding assistance from LCAD/COMSEC, is the Commonwealth Criminal Law Library (http://www.commonlii.org/crimlaw/) which brings together criminal law resources from all Commonwealth countries in one convenient searchable location, and updates the service daily from the databases of all LIIs involved in CommonLII.

How can Commonwealth countries assist CommonLII's development?

With funding secured for the next phase of development, the priority of CommonLII will be facilitating the efficient provision of case law, legislation, treaties, law journals, law reform reports and other legal data from Commonwealth countries, so that the creation of databases can be expanded and automated. To further the 2005 Ghana resolution of the Commonwealth Law Ministers, AustLII would like to invite the Law Ministries, Courts, and other law agencies of Commonwealth countries, as well as publishers of law journals, to contact AustLII[8] to discuss how legal materials from their country could most efficiently be made available to CommonLII or to the appropriate local LII. With this assistance from Commonwealth law agencies, CommonLII can progress toward becoming a comprehensive source for the whole of the common law world.

[6]This Project was presented by the Legal Editor of the Commonwealth Law Bulletin to the Thirteenth Ordinary Meeting of the CARICOM Legal Affairs Committee in September 2009, where it received widespread support and at which the nomenclature 'CaribLII' was first mooted.

[7]Including partner University funding from the University of New South Wales, Macquarie University, the Australian National University, the University of Sydney, University of Technology, Sydney, and University of Western Sydney.

[8]See email addresses for authors.

Acknowledgements

Thanks to Kieran Hackshall at AustlII for development of many of the databases. Research on the copyright issues related to commons in legal information was assisted by Abi Paramaguru, Research Assistant to the Australian Research Council Linkage Project 'Unlocking IP'.

Notes on contributors

Graham Greenleaf is Professor of Law at the University of New South Wales (UNSW); Andrew Mowbray is Professor of Law at the University of Technology, Sydney (UTS); and Philip Chung is Executive Director of AustLII and Lecturer in Law at the University of Technology, Sydney.

Annex I

Declaration on Free Access to Law[9]

Legal information institutes of the world, meeting in Montreal, declare that:

- Public legal information from all countries and international institutions is part of the common heritage of humanity. Maximising access to this information promotes justice and the rule of law;
- Public legal information is digital common property and should be accessible to all on a non-profit basis and free of charge;
- Organisations such as legal information institutes have the right to publish public legal information and the government bodies that create or control that information should provide access to it so that it can be published by other parties.

Public legal information means legal information produced by public bodies that have a duty to produce law and make it public. It includes primary sources of law, such as legislation, case law and treaties, as well as various secondary (interpretative) public sources, such as reports on preparatory work and law reform, and resulting from boards of inquiry. It also includes legal documents created as a result of public funding.

Publicly funded secondary (interpretative) legal materials should be accessible for free but permission to republish is not always appropriate or possible. In particular free access to legal scholarship may be provided by legal scholarship repositories, legal information institutes or other means.

Legal information institutes:

- Publish via the internet public legal information originating from more than one public body;
- Provide free and anonymous public access to that information;
- Do not impede others from obtaining public legal information from its sources and publishing it; and
- Support the objectives set out in this Declaration.

All legal information institutes are encouraged to participate in regional or global free access to law networks.

Therefore, the legal information institutes agree:

- To promote and support free access to public legal information throughout the world, principally via the Internet;

---

[9]Montreal Declaration (2002) – Declaration on Free Access to Law, Montreal, 2002 (as amended), ⟨http://www.worldlii.org/worldlii/declaration/⟩.

- To recognise the primary role of local initiatives in free access publishing of their own national legal information;
- To cooperate in order to achieve these goals and, in particular, to assist organisations in developing countries to achieve these goals, recognising the reciprocal advantages that all obtain from access to each other's law;
- To help each other and to support, within their means, other organisations that share these goals with respect to:
    - Promotion, to governments and other organisations, of public policy conducive to the accessibility of public legal information;
    - Technical assistance, advice and training;
    - Development of open technical standards;
    - Academic exchange of research results.
- To meet at least annually, and to invite other organisations who are legal information institutes to subscribe to this declaration and join those meetings, according to procedures to be established by the parties to this Declaration;
- To provide to the end users of public legal information clear information concerning any conditions of re-use of that information, where this is feasible.

This declaration was made by legal information institutes meeting in Montreal in 2002, as amended at meetings in Sydney (2003), Paris (2004) and Montreal (2007).

Index